GOOD POEMS

AMERICAN PLACES

Selected and Introduced by

GARRISON KEILLOR

PENGUIN BOOKS

PENGUIN BOOKS

Published by the Penguin Group
Penguin Group (USA) Inc., 375 Hudson Street, New York, New York 10014, U.S.A.
Penguin Group (Canada), 90 Eglinton Avenue East, Suite 700, Toronto,
Ontario, Canada M4P 2Y3 (a division of Pearson Penguin Canada Inc.)
Penguin Books Ltd, 80 Strand, London WC2R 0RL, England
Penguin Ireland, 25 St. Stephen's Green, Dublin 2, Ireland (a division of Penguin Books Ltd)
Penguin Books Australia Ltd, 250 Camberwell Road, Camberwell,
Victoria 3124, Australia (a division of Pearson Australia Group Pty Ltd)
Penguin Books India Pvt Ltd, 11 Community Centre, Panchsheel Park, New Delhi – 110 017, India
Penguin Group (NZ), 67 Apollo Drive, Rosedale, Auckland 0632,
New Zealand (a division of Pearson New Zealand Ltd)
Penguin Books (South Africa) (Pty) Ltd, 24 Sturdee Avenue,
Rosebank, Johannesburg 2196, South Africa

Penguin Books Ltd, Registered Offices:
80 Strand, London WC2R 0RL, England

First published in the United States of America by Viking Penguin,
a member of Penguin Group (USA) Inc. 2011
Published in Penguin Books 2012

1 3 5 7 9 10 8 6 4 2

THE LIBRARY OF CONGRESS HAS CATALOGED THE HARDCOVER EDITION AS FOLLOWS:
Good poems, American places / selected and introduced by Garrison Keillor.
p. cm.
Includes indexes.
ISBN 978-0-670-02254-0 (hc.)
ISBN 978-0-14-312076-6 (pbk.)
1. American poetry.   2. United States—Poetry.   3. U.S. states—Poetry.   I. Keillor, Garrison.
PS595.U5G66 2011
811.008'035873—dc22   2011005088

Printed in the United States of America

ALWAYS LEARNING   PEARSON

To the tourists who like to look at this vast land and mingle with the citizenry and go home and tell about it

Thanks

Francesca Cavilia managed this book from its formation in stacks of paper to its final assembly, proofing, and binding, with the help of Ella Schovanec. Kathy Roach handled permissions. Stevie Beck and Bob Ashenmacher read proof. Laura Tisdel hovered over it, fanning it with her wings.

Contents

5. 2 X 2 X 2

6. A COMFORTING IMMENSITY

7. A SORT OF RAPTURE

8. ON THE AVENUE

9. SNOW

10. RESIDENTIAL

11. GOOD WORK

12. OUT WEST

13. SHOW BUSINESS

14. OCEAN BRINE

15. NEVER EXPECTED TO BE THERE

Introduction

Over the sofa in my childhood home hung an illuminated picture of a snow-capped mountain range at sunset, purchased at 50% off at Sears. Backlit by a 20-watt bulb—bright golds and greens and reddish browns, very snazzy—it shone handsomely, and when guests came we made sure to switch it on. Ten feet away, our picture window looked out on the front yard, a gravel road, a cornfield beyond, a too-familiar tableau. The illuminated picture, the sort that the Great Northern Railroad put on its posters, suggested to me the Venturing Spirit of the Bold Traveler and, to my mother, the handiwork of God. "How can you look at this and say there is no God?" she said. I (who had not said there is no God, though I had thought it numerous times) said, "And what about when you look at the desert?" To base one's faith on beautiful scenery is to leave oneself open to grave doubt if you should visit Oklahoma.

We lived in unmountainous Minnesota, and every summer we six kids and two parents climbed in the station wagon and headed west across the plains to visit relatives in the hills of Idaho and Washington, Dad at the wheel, Mother in the shotgun seat, a breadboard across her lap to make baloney sandwiches on so we wouldn't have to stop for meals and waste all that money. A car trip was an emotional high point for my hardworking carpenter/postal clerk father, not that he would've said so ever, but nonetheless we could feel his exhilaration when he swung the car onto the two-lane concrete ribbon of Highway 10 out of Anoka and headed west. I sat in the rearmost seat and watched for classmates on the street, hoping they'd spot us as they went about their humdrum lives—*the Travelling Keillors*—and in case anyone was looking, I struck a pose, arm on the open window, very casual, eyes forward, breeze in my hair, like Alan Ladd looking for Apaches.

Out on the open road, Dad maintained a steady 60 mph as eastbound semis blew past like ICBM missiles and my mother shuddered at each one, anticipating a screech of brakes and a ball of fire and (I suppose) Jesus holding out His hands and welcoming us to glory. We didn't listen to the radio. No need to. We sat quietly in our places and feasted on the passing tableau, stopping for the occasional historical marker (*In memory of Officers and soldiers who fell near this place fighting with the 7th United States Cavalry against Sioux Indians on the 25th and 26th of June, A.D. 1876*) and I said to myself the beautiful names of Montana and the Bitterroot Valley, Old Woman Peak and Blue Mountain, the Sapphire Mountains, the Mission range and Rattlesnake Creek. When we finally arrived at Aunt Edith and Uncle Edmund's farm, jammed up against steep mountain slopes on the banks of the St. Joe River, our brains were teeming with images—the majestic buttes, mountains like the ones on our living room wall, the grim taverns in western towns, the beat-up cars, weather-beaten frame houses with junky yards, no shade trees, and dirty-faced children peering out from behind a wire fence. Bleak poverty against a backdrop of movie splendor.

We were city people and Mother dressed us nicely so we felt slightly starched and prissy among cousins who raised cows and chickens and drove tractors, but we roughed ourselves up and blended in, which children have a knack for, and one astonishing afternoon, while the grown-ups were away at prayer meeting, cousin Chuck slid over and gave me the wheel of the Allis-Chalmers, a terrifying pleasure for a city kid, age 12, driving a massive tractor up a steep twisting dirt road through stands of tall pines, the great black treads turning, the engine throbbing beneath me and, far beyond, the forested peaks mounting into the sky and the road curving into the folds of the foothills. This was not about faith in God. It was about being in an enormous moment, a cautious boy inhaling the balsam air, suddenly promoted from passenger to driver, putting my sneaker down on the gas pedal, shifting up to second gear, thrilled by the pounding pulsation of the wheel, the steep incline, Chuck hanging on to my shoulders, and if I had written a good poem (*Gunning The Engine Up The Mountain, Idaho, 1954*) I might have included it in this book, but I didn't.

This is a book of poems in which the poet simply is carried away by a particular place in America: a canyon in Arizona, the town dump, the ballpark, the barbershop, the suburban backyard, Boulder Dam, Route 66, the Big Horn Mountains, the lobby of the Algonquin, a cornfield in autumn, a snowy gravel road, a shopping mall, seat 23D on a flight to Los Angeles, a bridge over the Lac Qui Parle River, a laundromat, a town in Kansas, Ed's New York apartment, a 100-year-old farmhouse, a soldier's grave in Virginia, a circle of farmers squatting and conversing and tracing figures in the dust with a stick. Carried away by some ordinary American reality that the poet stares at for a long little while and loses track of mortality, the disappointment of midlife, loneliness, the pain caused by the bad daddy or the clueless lover or the irritable children, and renders a memoir of the place in that moment. This is a lovely simple human thing. The poet (who may be famous for his multilayered recontextualized decolonized unhegemonic antipatrimonial and self-deconstructed cantos that seminars of shriveled midgets are busy pondering) takes off his Distinguished Poet hat and says, *Let me tell you what happened to me this one time, and it was snowing and my lover and I lay in the tent and heard the silence, the silence was audible* in the same way that anybody else would tell about a running catch in deep right field or being nibbled by minnows in a creek or some other god blessed transcendent moment arising from a specific place and time.

Kenneth Rexroth got carried away by the high Sierras—hiking and camping saved him from being just another angry old San Francisco radical. May Swenson was a Utah Mormon who moved to

New York for the freedom to love women and her gratitude to the city breathes in her tender snapshots of MoMA, the A train, and Ed's apartment. Jim Harrison was carried away by the Arizona desert, Maxine Kumin by her hilltop farm in New Hampshire, Charles Bukowski by the Santa Anita racetrack. Other poets are transported by a hardware store and its vast glossary or a grove where ancient cars sink into the earth, a small town in Kansas, or the memory of a grandmother hurling a long arc of dishwater from a basin. And of course everyone is astonished by snowfall, and so the book includes a whole section devoted to that, as well as nakedness, a memorable experience always.

The solace of the real world: you step out of your jumbled inner life and into the woods along the river and your heart lifts. This sort of thing happens to millions of people every day, so why not to poets? When we sat brooding over life's insults, Mother said, "Go. Get yourself outdoors or I'll give you something to cry about." And we got ourselves outdoors and the neighbor kids were riding their bikes no-handed down the street and waving sparklers and their dog was yapping at the back wheels and their dad was weaving lines of spray from a hose over his flower beds. He shot some spray their way and they squealed, and that little carnival of light and noise took your mind off your troubles. The real world trumps the imaginary. They may not tell you this in Poetry Writing 101: the dear readers, bless their hearts, have their bullshit detectors turned up high when reading a poem and usually those detectors start beeping by the second line. When they read John Hollander's ode to movie-going in Manhattan, and he mentions the RKO Colonial, Loew's Lincoln Square, Thalia, Riviera, Carlton, Edison, Nemo—*those had better be real movie theaters, not made-up names*—or else the book slaps shut. In James Wright's "From a Bus Window in Central Ohio, Just Before a Thunder Shower," we believe that that is a real farmer and real Holsteins and that we're in Ohio and not in Saskatchewan. When Donald Hall says Newberry's store in Franklin, NH, with its lunch counter and all, has closed, we would be dismayed if we learned it was still open and had never served "beans and franks and coleslaw" but specialized in stir-fried tofu lightly drizzled with avocado mist.

Americans are impatient with riddles and so they give poetry a wide berth, knowing from Miss Fernwood's 8th grade English class that a page of writing with an uneven right margin means a series of jokes with no punch lines, a puzzle with no right answers. And Americans have an irreverent streak: we sit in church hoping someone will fart. Poetry is a hushed chapel in which the poet sighs and the congregation must sigh along with her. And in this chapel, nobody ever farts. The gases are absorbed in the heart and emitted verbally.

What Miss Fernwood did not say is that it is permissible not to appreciate the poem even if it is Emily or Walt or T.S. This happens all the time, even among the learned. My old friend the late distinguished novelist J.F. Powers loathed Whitman from the depths of his dark Irish heart and if you admitted to sort of liking even parts of "Song of Myself" he would step away from you as if you had head lice and your hair was moving. It's hard to enforce "appreciation" of poetry. The more reverent the teacher the more restless the pupils. What helps is to find the humanity of the poet—to visit Emily's house in Amherst, to climb the steep stairs to the front room with the small square table by the window where she sat in her divine privacy and took endless pains rewriting—rewiring—her verses.

Anyway.

Paging through the unreadable work of various highly honored poets, one longs for a little humanity, a little attention paid to their surroundings. Some grit, some spark, maybe an ode to the old hometown, to the marble majesty of Colburn-Hilliard Men's Clothing and the bounty of Benzian Furniture and Amidore's Appliances, the sweet solace of Shadick's Soda Fountain, and the old ladies trying on black slacks in Dedrick's Department Store, rather than a soliloquy on the brevity of life. Mortality is pretty much the same for everybody—*The end comes too soon! Too soon!*—and Shakespeare's sonnets set a high standard here, do they not? So one is grateful if, instead of playing that old lament, the poet pays attention to the astonishment that awaits on a particular fall day in Missoula, Montana.

There are handsome monastic poets who write from seclusion, often about the sacred ineffable, and there are street poets who pick up shiny objects, some of them plastic or cellophane, and in this book you'll find the Milky Way, snow, the sky, mountains, and also Dr Pepper, Milk Duds, Walmart, Winn-Dixie, Baryshnikov, a Cherry Queen in northwestern Ohio, Velveeta, Avenue C, a 1937 Chevy pickup, the town of Conception Junction, a blue neon insect electrocuter, chainsaws, Voyager II, and the Cowgirl Luncheonette in Seattle. There are daffodils too (a few) and moonlight and generic sunsets, but also the Dodgers, Tina Turner, a seal named Earl, the Russian Tea Room, Minnehaha Falls, and the dishpan bell of the yellow trolley.

In the classic tradition, poets strove for universality, and so Emily Dickinson did not tell us if the Horses whose heads turned toward Eternity were Percherons or Shetland ponies, nor if the narrow fellow in the grass was a black snake or a garter. Nor did Robert Frost have a specific boy swing on those birches, wearing U.S. Keds and blowing Fleer's bubblegum while singing "Alexander's Ragtime Band." Serious poets did not step in the mundane for fear it would date them, diminish the universality, and perhaps also because—well, because America was rather *vulgar* with all those asphalt parking lots and shopping malls—and poets felt obliged to rise above the vulgar immediate, up to the distant ideal.

The upward-striving poets are happy enough to drop European places into their work—*In a café in Verona, I suddenly thought of my father*—romantic places (Rome, Genoa, Venice, Paris, of course) being preferable to Sweden or Germany—which paid off nicely: the poet immediately elevated himself by being in Paris, and he could write with a freer hand, knowing American readers could not hold him so closely to account as if the poem were set in the middle of Manhattan.

The world is our consolation. When in disgrace with fortune and men's eyes, we get into our car and drive. It's a big country. You can drive from the rocky coast of Maine, down to the stone Victorian solemnity of Buffalo to Manhattan and the statue of Daniel Webster in Central Park, and south to the Methodist camp meeting at Ocean Grove and its 7000-seat wooden tabernacle and tent cottages. To Philadelphia with the statue of William Penn on the peak of City Hall at the foot of Broad Street where the 14th Pennsylvania Regiment formed up in 1861 and where on New Year's Day cops and firemen, teamsters and other manly men dress up in sequined costumes and feathers and golden slippers to strut in the Mummers Parade. And Bethlehem on the Lehigh River in Pennsylvania, home to Bethlehem Steel, which made the beams for the Golden Gate Bridge and much of the skyline of Manhattan and then collapsed like a pile of bricks. Work your way south to the Virginia Tidewater where the Potomac, the York, the James, and the Rappahannock rivers flow into Chesapeake Bay and where tobacco was first raised, the grim drudgery of which led to the importation of slaves from Africa in 1619, which made us the country we are today. No slaves, no jazz, less juice in the language. West to Nashville where tall men in cowboy hats and big shiny belt buckles stride along Honky Tonk Row and waitresses call you Darling. Head south, listening to black preachers Sunday morning on the AM radio, to Georgia and the magnolias of Columbus, across the Chattahoochee west to New Orleans, the Crescent City, where the Mississippi is half a mile wide and where you find Faubourg Tremé (pronounced Foe-boorg Tre-may), next to the French Quarter, settled by free slaves in the late eighteenth century, and upriver to Memphis and Beale Street, St. Louis and Tennessee Williams, Dubuque, St. Paul, and over to the elegance of Milwaukee, home of Pabst, Blatz, Schlitz; where, in 1903, William S. Harley and Arthur Davidson mounted an engine on a bicycle. To Peoria on the Illinois River, a factory town (bicycles, bags, forklift trucks, washing machines, flyswatters, brick and tile, flour, rope, barrels, traffic lights, caskets, barbed wire, and Caterpillar heavy equipment) where Abraham Lincoln came on October 10, 1857, to defend a woman named Melissa Goings, charged with killing her husband with a stick of firewood during a quarrel.

Lincoln entered a plea of not guilty on her behalf and after a whispered conversation with the defendant, she left and was never seen in Peoria again. When asked what they'd been talking about, Lincoln said, "She wanted to know where she could get a good drink of water and I told her there was some mighty good water in Tennessee." From Illinois, you can ride the California Zephyr, the most beautiful train trip in America, through the density of South Side Chicago, the little frame and brick houses squeezed together behind tiny yards on what once was a swamp and an Army camp where 6000 Confederate prisoners died of smallpox and dysentery and are buried in a mass grave in Oak Woods cemetery. The train chugs across Iowa and the exhilarating emptiness of Nebraska and through Denver and the Rockies and the high desert valley of Reno on the Truckee River and Lake Tahoe, where the air is so pure, Mark Twain said, "it could restore an Egyptian mummy to his pristine vigor . . . maybe not the oldest and driest mummies, but the fresher ones."

You could turn north to the ferries of Puget Sound and ride the Coast Starlight south through the Cascades to San Francisco and Fort Mason on the Bay, where millions of men shipped out for World War II and the Korean War and Vietnam, its old supply hangars now the sites of boutiques and restaurants and craft fairs. Fly off to the semitropical archipelago of Hawaii, birthplace of Barack Obama, and along the way, no matter how weary or discouraged you may be, sick of politics and phony piety, media monkeytalk, TV comedy, lousy food, stupefying music, sick of yourself and your bad life choices, you will come upon the places in these poems, the country store with the freezer full of blueberries, the "waters rushing among the wooden piers" of a bridge, the "salt, salt smell of the thick sea air" and the driftwood fire on the beach, the boy in the clean undershirt at the Laundromat, the candy store and the girl with breathless breasts, the softball players crying *Hum baby hey baby hum hey,* a truckload of butter on the freeway, the sack dresses and Sansabelt slacks at the family reunion, the solemn-sweet pipes of the organ, the broken-down cars in the dead weeds, roadside wisteria, a small bridge in the moonlight, snow falling in the morning streets of Chicago, the locker-room chalkboard where the coach wrote *Execution,* the cold-creamed shrimp soup in the Court of the Two Sisters restaurant, the fireflies under the stars, the line of telephone poles across Kansas, the arrowheads in the meadow above the Pate Valley, the yellow schoolbus in Wyoming, the cowboy on the bucking bronco named Firecracker, the rattlesnake and its babies in the hole under the juniper stump, the oil rigs off Long Beach, the avalanche ride at Universal Studios, the couple kissing at Gate C22, a rainstorm in Seattle, or the starfish in the tide pools. It's all in here, it's all out there.

America

My country, 'tis of thee,
Sweet land of liberty, of thee I sing;
Land where my fathers died,
Land of the pilgrims' pride,
From every mountainside let freedom ring!

Let music swell the breeze,
And ring from all the trees sweet freedom's song;
Let mortal tongues awake;
Let all that breathe partake;
Let rocks their silence break, the sound prolong.

O had I wings to fly
I'd mount up to the sky
With a big wahoo.
I'd wear a spangled suit,
A hat with lots of fruit,
And pull my parachute,
Red white and blue.

Sweet land of poetry,
Rhythm and harmony,
Sweet land of slang.
Doo-wop hip-hop kerflop,
Jelly roll and soda pop,
Wop bop a loo shbop
Shang a lang lang lang.

My country of romance
Where Fred and Ginger dance,
The Coasters sing.
God gave us rock and roll
And blues to make us whole
And give us heart and soul—
Long may it swing.

Beloved country thee,
May it be ever free
For rich and poor.
And may Miss Liberty
Standing beside the sea
Hold up her torch for me,
An open door.

1

ON THE ROAD

In a Train

Robert Bly

There has been a light snow.
Dark car tracks move in out of the darkness.
I stare at the train window marked with soft dust.
I have awakened at Missoula, Montana, utterly happy.

Locomotion

Philip Bryant

I heard the
locomotion behind
the album by Monk my father
was playing.
The finely tuned
machine humming like
a top, purring like a kitten.

The first time I
saw the Santa Fe "Super Chief"
at Union Station in Chicago,
gleaming as a silver bullet
carrying the blue uniformed
conductor who gave a low whistle
and "All Aboard" for places as far away as Kansas,
Laredo, Tucson, Las Vegas, Palm Springs.

At that point
I knew it all had
something to do with jazz music.
The slow hiss of
the engine, the steam
let out by the jowls of the locomotive,
and the massive, muscular wheels turning
slowly counterclockwise to the engine's beat

Come on Baby Do the Locomotion
Come on Baby Do the Locomotion With Me

heading out onto the open tracks,
that smoke-blown phrase repeated
over and over in my head through the years,
as miles of the real American landscape
began, slowly, to unfold.

Small Towns Are Passing

Wesley McNair

Small towns are passing
into the rearview
mirrors of our cars.
The white houses
are moving away,
wrapping trees
around themselves,
and stores are taking
their gas pumps
down the street
backwards. Just like that
whole families picnicking
on their lawns tilt
over the hill,
and kids on bikes
ride toward us
off the horizon,
leaving no trace
of where they have gone.
Signs turn back and start
after them. Packs of mailboxes,
like dogs, chase them
around corner after corner.

From a Bus Window in Central Ohio, Just Before a Thunder Shower

James Wright

Cribs loaded with roughage huddle together
Before the north clouds.
The wind tiptoes between poplars.
The silver maple leaves squint
Toward the ground.
An old farmer, his scarlet face
Apologetic with whiskey, swings back a barn door
And calls a hundred black-and-white Holsteins
From the clover field.

On the Road, between Toledo & Cincinnati, Late June

Sebastian Matthews

Somewhere dead center in the day's drive
through this relentlessly flat state, the sky
darkens and fills up deepend blue,
and the word 'rain' comes to your lips
twenty seconds before the first waterballoon
droplets hit; and before you can think
or turn and say 'storm' here it comes
spilling out of its box like a load of grain.
The woman in the passenger seat
of a raggedly elegant convertible, top down,
laughs merrily, purse held over her head.
Motorcycles cluster under the awnings
of bridges, five, six, a whole family of Harleys:
Middle Americans for a brief spell
hobos, gathering around the fire
of manageable happenstance. We'll all
make it through. No twister coming to life
out of the yellowing swirl. No pile-up crash
in our cards. The rain subsiding, wipers
knocked back to intermittent, you drive on
through the burgeoning heat: crows
congregating in the backyards of trees,
fireworks stockpiling in the beds of pickups,
young girls towed behind speedboats
in inner tubes, shouting to each other

as they pass over the rotting corpse
of a deer that, a year-rounder told,
finally fell after a long winter
through the melting ice and settled
uneasily on the lake bottom.

Over Ohio

Michael Blumenthal

You can say what you want about the evils of technology
and the mimicry of birds: *I love it.* I love the sheer,
unexpurgated *hubris* of it, I love the beaten egg whites
of clouds hovering beneath me, this ephemeral Hamlet
of believing in man's grandeur. You can have all that
talk about the holiness of nature and the second Babylon.
You can stay shocked about the future all you want,
reminisce about the beauties of midwifery. I'll take this
anyday, this sweet imitation of Mars and Jupiter, this
sitting still at 600 mph like a jet-age fetus. I want to
go on looking at the moon for the rest of my life and seeing
footsteps. I want to keep flying, even for short distances,
like here between Columbus and Toledo on Air Wisconsin:
an Andean condor sailing over Ohio, above the factories,
above the dust and the highways and the miserable tires.

The Sacred

Stephen Dunn

After the teacher asked if anyone had
    a sacred place
and the students fidgeted and shrank

in their chairs, the most serious of them all
    said it was his car,
being in it alone, his tape deck playing

things he'd chosen, and others knew the truth
    had been spoken
and began speaking about their rooms,

their hiding places, but the car kept coming up,
    the car in motion,
music filling it, and sometimes one other person

who understood the bright altar of the dashboard
    and how far away
a car could take him from the need

to speak, or to answer, the key
    in having a key
and putting it in, and going.

Driving Toward the Lac Qui Parle River

Robert Bly

I

I am driving; it is dusk; Minnesota.
The stubble field catches the last growth of sun.
The soybeans are breathing on all sides.
Old men are sitting before their houses on carseats
In the small towns. I am happy,
The moon rising above the turkey sheds.

II

The small world of the car
Plunges through the deep fields of the night,
On the road from Willmar to Milan.
This solitude covered with iron
Moves through the fields of night
Penetrated by the noise of crickets.

III

Nearly to Milan, suddenly a small bridge,
And water kneeling in the moonlight.
In small towns the houses are built right on the ground;
The lamplight falls on all fours in the grass.
When I reach the river, the full moon covers it;
A few people are talking, low, in a boat.

Campbellsburg

Reid Bush

Driving State Road 60 northwest out of Salem,

10 miles out—
and 10 before you come to Spring Mill Park—

off to your right—for just a blacktop minute—
is Campbellsburg,

which was a town
when the man you were named for had his store there,

but a glance through your window reveals it's now gray
        abandonment—
ugly sag and fall.

And you wonder who lives there now
and how anyone
even to have a brick store all his own
ever could.

But nothing about it matters to you half as much as that your dad
came in from that hill farm to the north
to go to high school there.

And that's what you always point out to whoever's with you in the
        car.

And through the years what all your passengers have had in
 common is
no matter how you point it out
they can't care enough.

Homesteader

John Haag

The '37 Chevy pickup, retired to a rest
of rust and thistles, sloughed off its front
wheels—the better to munch the sod and
ruminate on great loads hauled: lumber,
a keg of nails, the tools and paint
for their first frame farmhouse, then
the bed, a castiron cookstove with its
clatter of pans, plus the barbwire and
feedbags, a pump . . . later, kids
and hogs and heifers to the county fair.
Lasting out the War to End All Wars, and
then Korea, she earned her ease, turned
out to pasture by the old woodlot, where
time and the weather wrought a work of art,
making her a monument to herself.

Moment

C.G. Hanzlicek

The moments pass,
Moment by moment,
Like they're on a fast track to somewhere
Worse than Oblivion Depot,
But once in a while,
On a lucky day,
The bullet train stops
And lets you on board.
This day was solid overcast
Except for one thin band
On the eastern horizon,
Where it looked like the gallery
For Chinese landscapes was open for viewing.
The scroll was painted lengthwise,
A long stretch of snowfields
In the high Sierra pure white
In the new sun.
Most days the cloud cover
Will drop back down in minutes,
But we decided to drive east
Until the curtain fell.
One road led into another,
And still the scene held.
Finally we were in foothills
Smeared with mustard flower and fiddleneck,

On a paved road that turned to gravel
At the gate across someone's driveway.
I wonder what it feels like
To come home each evening
To the literal end of the road?
We turned around.
At the crest of the first hill,
A meadowlark perched on a strand of wire
No more than five feet from the car.
He had the yellowest breast
I'd seen on a lark, so I braked
And lowered the window for a clearer look.
He squirted out a quick
White poop as if in greeting,
And then began what may be
The loveliest bird song of all.
Another joined him and then another,
And Dianne rolled down her window,
And I killed the engine,
And suddenly the songs of a whole field
Of larks, fifty of them maybe,
Filled the car.
Fifty meadowlarks singing to each other,
Or maybe singing one to one,
In the early morning,
In the middle of our lives,
In the middle of the San Joaquin Valley.
There were only two houses nearby,
And for a moment I envied
The people who lived there,
In the middle of that sound each morning,
But then I thought maybe it was we

Who should be envied,
For whom the larks sang deeper,
And even, stretching all the way from there
To this very moment,
Sang longer.

Flying Lesson

Julia Kasdorf

Over a tray of spent plates, I confessed
to the college president my plans to go East,
to New York, which I'd not really seen,
though it seemed the right place
for a sophomore as sullen and restless
as I had become on that merciless
Midwestern plain. He slowly stroked
a thick cup and described the nights
when, a theology teacher in Boston, he'd fly
a tiny plane alone out over the ocean,
each time pressing farther into the dark
until the last moment, when he'd turn
toward the coast's bright spine, how he loved
the way the city glittered beneath him
as he glided gracefully toward it,
engine gasping, fuel needle dead on empty,
the way sweat dampened the back of his neck
when he climbed from the cockpit, giddy.
Buttoned up in my cardigan, young, willing
to lose everything, how could I see generosity
or warning? But now that I'm out here,
his advice comes so clear: fling yourself
farther, and a bit farther each time,
but darling, don't drop.

Toward the Verrazano

Stephen Dunn

Up from South Jersey and the low persistent
pines, pollution curls into the sky
like dark cast-off ribbons
and the part of us that's pure camera,
that loves funnel clouds and blood
on a white dress, is satisfied.
At mile 127, no trace of a tree now,
nothing but concrete and high tension
wires, we hook toward the Outerbridge
past Arthur Kill Road where garbage trucks
work the largest landfill in the world.
The windscreens are littered, gorgeous
with rotogravure sections, torn love
letters, mauve once-used tissues. The gulls
dip down like addicts, rise like angels.
Soon we're in traffic, row houses, a college
we've never heard of stark as an asylum.
In the distance there it is, the crown
of this back way in, immense, silvery,
and in no time we're suspended
out over the Narrows by a logic linked
to faith, so accustomed to the miraculous
we hardly speak, and when we do
it's with those words found on picture postcards
from polite friends with nothing to say.

Night Journey

Theodore Roethke

Now as the train bears west,
Its rhythm rocks the earth,
And from my Pullman berth
I stare into the night
While others take their rest.
Bridges of iron lace,
A suddenness of trees,
A lap of mountain mist
All cross my line of sight,
Then a bleak wasted place,
And a lake below my knees.
Full on my neck I feel
The straining at a curve;
My muscles move with steel,
I wake in every nerve.
I watch a beacon swing
From dark to blazing bright;
We thunder through ravines
And gullies washed with light.
Beyond the mountain pass
Mist deepens on the pane;
We rush into a rain
That rattles double glass.
Wheels shake the roadbed stone,
The pistons jerk and shove,
I stay up half the night
To see the land I love.

Folsom Prison Blues

Johnny Cash

I hear that train a-comin'; it's rollin' 'round the bend,
And I ain't seen the sunshine since I don't know when.
I'm stuck at Folsom Prison and time keeps draggin' on.
But that train keeps rollin' on down to San Antone.

When I was just a baby, my mama told me, "Son,
Always be a good boy; don't ever play with guns."
But I shot a man in Reno, just to watch him die.
When I hear that whistle blowin' I hang my head and cry.

I bet there's rich folk eatin' in a fancy dining car.
They're prob'ly drinkin' coffee and smokin' big cigars,
But I know I had it comin', I know I can't be free,
But those people keep a-movin', and that's what tortures me.

Well, if they freed me from this prison, if that railroad train
        was mine,
I bet I'd move it over a little farther down the line,
Far from Folsom Prison, that's where I want to stay,
And I'd let that lonesome whistle blow my blues away.

Bums at Breakfast

David Wagoner

Daily, the bums sat down to eat in our kitchen.
They seemed to be whatever the day was like:
If it was hot or cold, they were hot or cold;
If it was wet, they came in dripping wet.
One left his snowy shoes on the back porch
But his socks stuck to the clean linoleum,
And one, when my mother led him to the sink,
Wrung out his hat instead of washing his hands.

My father said they'd made a mark on the house,
A hobo's sign on the sidewalk, pointing the way.
I hunted everywhere, but never found it.
It must have said, "It's only good in the morning—
When the husband's out." My father knew by heart
Lectures on Thrift and Doggedness,
But he was always either working or sleeping.
My mother didn't know any advice.

They ate their food politely, with old hands,
Not looking around, and spoke in short, plain answers.
Sometimes they said what they'd been doing lately
Or told us what was wrong; but listening hard,
I broke their language into secret codes:
Their *east* meant *west*, their *job* meant *walking and walking*,
Their *money* meant *danger*, *home* meant *running and hiding*,
Their *father* and *mother* were different kinds of weather.

Dumbly, I watched them leave by the back door,
Their pockets empty as a ten-year-old's;
Yet they looked twice as rich, being full of breakfast.
I carried mine like a lump all the way to school.
When I was growing hungry, where would they be?
None ever came twice. Never to lunch or dinner.
They were always starting fresh in the fresh morning.
I dreamed of days that stopped at the beginning.

Cottonwoods

Phebe Hanson

In the cottonwood grove
behind Dahl's farm
the eyes of rusting cars
stare at me before
I crawl into them,
pretend I am driving;
power flows from the wheels,
I believe I am in control,
forget my mother's heart
lies fading in a little bedroom
beyond the rows of corn.

They have sent me away
from her dying
to play in the grove,
to whisper into the ears of corn
towering above me
as I sit between the rows
reading her letters
which say she misses me,
even though it is quieter without me
and my brother fighting.
He has brought her a goldfish
from the little pond
beside the pergola house
and laid it on her stomach.

Years later I return to the grove,
where the cottonwood trees
have grown scrawny,
but the old cars are still there,
their eyes stare at me,
unseeing and dead.

Driving Through the Poconos, Route 80, 1:30 A.M., Snow

William Matthews

I pass the big rigs on the upgrades;
they measle me with roadslush on the downslopes.
Skeins of snowflakes waver in my headlights

like curtains in a draft. Of course I can't see
the swatches of black ice I speed across,
but I can feel a slur—a tiny, stifled

shimmy, faster than a thought—in my rear
tires. File cabinets and mattresses hurtle
downhill. Stroudsburg: 32 miles.

Enough butter to slather a county surges
past me. We bottom out. Carting a few
books and an extra pair of shoes, I pass

the butter. Semis doze in the rest areas,
the orange cab lights stippled by snow,
while we who are close enough to sleep

to keep on driving toward it, keep on
driving toward it, although we're neither
here (Stroudsburg: 11 miles) nor there.

Driving at Night

Sheila Packa

Up north, the dashboard lights of the family car
gleam in memory, the radio
plays to itself as I drive
my father plied the highways
while my mother talked, she tried to hide
that low lilt, that Finnish brogue,
in the back seat, my sisters and I
our eyes always tied to the Big Dipper
I watch it still
on summer evenings, as the fireflies stream
above the ditches and moths smack
into the windshield and the wildlife's
red eyes bore out from the dark forests
we flew by, then scattered like the last bit of star
light years before.
It's like a different country, the past
we made wishes on unnamed falling stars
that I've forgotten, that maybe were granted
because I wished for love.

Top Down

Fred Weil Jr.

I get behind the wheel of my automobile and drive around town, top down, good to be alive. You in the front seat feet up on the dashboard, a case of beer and the gearshift on the floor. Tall pine trees and morning glory vines, pink stucco drive-in under the neon signs. Carhop walks up, I say "Cokes and ice. Hamburgers well-done, onions, bucket of fries."

I love you from your hairdo to your bare feet. Green bikini and skin so clean and sweet. Tires humming on a summertime afternoon. We'll get old someday but no time soon. Susie Q, you and I twenty-two years old and singing along with our song on the radio. It goes, "Sh-bop sh-bop, yeah yeah, hey hey. Driving round town with the top down on a summer day."

Fifteen

William Stafford

South of the bridge on Seventeenth
I found back of the willows one summer
day a motorcycle with engine running
as it lay on its side, ticking over
slowly in the high grass. I was fifteen.

I admired all that pulsing gleam, the
shiny flanks, the demure headlights
fringed where it lay; I led it gently
to the road and stood with that
companion, ready and friendly. I was fifteen.

We could find the end of a road, meet
the sky on out Seventeenth. I thought about
hills, and patting the handle got back a
confident opinion. On the bridge we indulged
a forward feeling, a tremble. I was fifteen.

Thinking, back farther in the grass I found
the owner, just coming to, where he had flipped
over the rail. He had blood on his hand, was pale—
I helped him walk to his machine. He ran his hand
over it, called me good man, roared away.

I stood there, fifteen.

Hard River

James Finnegan

I pulled back
the jaundiced curtains
of the room rented
for four weeks in Wichita.
I didn't care
that the only thing I could see
from the window was the highway,
because I would watch the highway
the way I used to watch the river
with a six of beer and nowhere to go
after work, just watch
the cars and trucks
flow on and on, heading home
or to work or nowhere in particular,
knowing out there somewhere
someone was listening to the radio,
the same station I was listening to
with this man talking, just talking
into space, wavelengths over furrows
in the wide stretches of farmland,
knowing no one cares
about what he's saying,
still he talks and syllables and seconds
and dust settle like silt in the open air,
a child asleep across the backseat
of a car, tires throbbing over

slabs of pavement, no spare
in the trunk and two hundred miles
from here to wherever is there
on the hard river that carries them along
and if they're lucky
takes them home.

Driving West in 1970

Robert Bly

My dear children, do you remember the morning
When we climbed into the old Plymouth
And drove west straight toward the Pacific?

We were all the people there were.
We followed Dylan's songs all the way west.
It was Seventy; the war was over, almost;

And we were driving to the sea.
We had closed the farm, tucked in
The flap, and we were eating the honey

Of distance and the word "there."
*Oh whee, we're gonna fly
Down into the easy chair.* We sang that

Over and over. That's what the early
Seventies were like. We weren't afraid.
And a hole had opened in the world.

We laughed at Las Vegas.
There was enough gaiety
For all of us, and ahead of us was

The ocean. *Tomorrow's
The day my bride's gonna come.*
And the war was over, almost.

Mambo Cadillac

Barbara Hamby

Drive me to the edge in your Mambo Cadillac,
    turn left at the graveyard and gas that baby, the black
night ringing with its holy roller scream. I'll clock
    you on the highway at three a.m., amen, brother, smack
the road as hard as we can, because I'm gonna crack
    the world in two, make a hoodoo soup with chicken necks,
a gumbo with a plutonium roux, a little snack
    before the dirt and jalapeño stew that will shuck
the skin right off your slinky hips, Mr. I'm-not-stuck
    in-a-middle-class-prison-with-someone-I-hate sack
of blues. Put on your highwire shoes, Mr. Right, and stick
    with me, 'cause I'm going nowhere fast, the burlesque
queen of this dim scene, I want to feel the wind, the Glock
    in my mouth, going south, down-by-the-riverside shock
of the view. Take me to Shingles Fried Chicken Shack
    in your Mambo Cadillac. I was gone, but I'm back
for good this time. I've taken a shine to daylight. Crank
    up that radio, baby, put on some dance music
and shake your moneymaker, sweetheart, rev it up to mach
    two. I'm talking to you, Mr. Magoo. Sit up, check
out that blonde with the leopard print tattoo. O she'll lick
    the sugar right off your doughnut and bill you, too, speak
French while she do the do. Parlez-vous français? Okay, pick
    me up tonight at ten in your Mambo Cadillac
'cause we got a date with the devil, so fill the tank
    with high-octane rhythm and blues, sugar cane, and shark

bait, too. We got some miles to cover, me and you, think
       Chile, Argentina, Peru. Take some time off work,
'cause we're gonna be gone a lot longer than a week
       or two. Is this D-day or Waterloo? White or black—
it's up to you. We'll be in Mexico tonight. Pack
       a razor, pack some glue. Things fall apart off the track,
and that's where we'll be, baby, in your Mambo Cadillac,
       'cause you're looking for love, but I'm looking for a wreck.

2

A WARM SUMMER

On the Back Porch

Dorianne Laux

The cat calls for her dinner.
On the porch I bend and pour
brown soy stars into her bowl,
stroke her dark fur.
It's not quite night.
Pinpricks of light in the eastern sky.
Above my neighbor's roof, a transparent
moon, a pink rag of cloud.
Inside my house are those who love me.
My daughter dusts biscuit dough.
And there's a man who will lift my hair
in his hands, brush it
until it throws sparks.
Everything is just as I've left it.
Dinner simmers on the stove.
Glass bowls wait to be filled
with gold broth. Sprigs of parsley
on the cutting board.
I want to smell this rich soup, the air
around me going dark, as stars press
their simple shapes into the sky.
I want to stay on the back porch
while the world tilts
toward sleep, until what I love
misses me, and calls me in.

Summer Kitchen ·

Donald Hall

In June's high light she stood at the sink
    With a glass of wine,
And listened for the bobolink,
And crushed garlic in late sunshine.

I watched her cooking, from my chair.
    She pressed her lips
Together, reached for kitchenware,
And tasted sauce from her fingertips.

"It's ready now. Come on," she said.
    "You light the candle."
We ate, and talked, and went to bed,
And slept. It was a miracle.

A Warm Summer in San Francisco

Carolyn Miller

Although I watched and waited for it every day,
somehow I missed it, the moment when everything reached
the peak of ripeness. It wasn't at the solstice; that was only
the time of the longest light. It was sometime after that, when
the plants had absorbed all that sun, had taken it into themselves
for food and swelled to the height of fullness. It was in July,
in a dizzy blaze of heat and fog, when on some nights
it was too hot to sleep, and the restaurants set half their tables
on the sidewalks; outside the city, down the coast,
the Milky Way floated overhead, and shooting stars
fell from the sky over the ocean. One day the garden
was almost overwhelmed with fruition:
My sweet peas struggled out of the raised bed onto the mulch
of laurel leaves and bark and pods, their brilliantly colored
sunbonnets of rose and stippled pink, magenta and deep purple
pouring out a perfume that was almost oriental. Black-eyed Susans
stared from the flower borders, the orange cherry tomatoes
were sweet as candy, the corn fattened in its swaths of silk,
hummingbirds spiraled by in pairs, the bees gave up
and decided to live in the lavender. At the market,
surrounded by black plums and rosy plums and sugar prunes
and white-fleshed peaches and nectarines, perfumey melons
and mangos, purple figs in green plastic baskets,
clusters of tiny Champagne grapes and piles of red-black cherries
and apricots freckled and streaked with rose, I felt tears
come into my eyes, absurdly, because I knew
that summer had peaked and was already passing

away. I felt very close then to understanding
the mystery; it seemed to me that I almost knew
what it meant to be alive, as if my life had swelled
to some high moment of response, as if I could
reach out and touch the season, as if I were inside
its body, surrounded by sweet pulp and juice,
shimmering veins and ripened skin.

Reverence

Julie Cadwallader-Staub

The air vibrated
with the sound of cicadas
on those hot Missouri nights after sundown
when the grown-ups gathered on the wide back lawn,
sank into their slung-back canvas chairs
tall glasses of iced tea beading in the heat

and we sisters chased fireflies
reaching for them in the dark
admiring their compact black bodies
their orange stripes and seeking antennas
as they crawled to our fingertips
and clicked open into the night air.

In all the days and years that have followed,
I don't know that I've ever experienced
that same utter certainty of the goodness of life
that was as palpable
as the sound of the cicadas on those nights:

my sisters running around with me in the dark,
the murmur of the grown-ups' voices,
the way reverence mixes with amazement
to see such a small body
emit so much light.

Produce

Debra Allbery

No mountains or ocean, but we had orchards
in northwestern Ohio, roadside stands
telling what time of summer: strawberries,
corn, apples—and festivals to parade
the crops, a Cherry Queen, a Sauerkraut Dance.
Somebody would block off a street in town,
put up beer tents and a tilt-a-whirl.

Our first jobs were picking berries.
We'd ride out early in the back of a pickup—
kids my age, and migrants, and old men
we called bums in sour flannel shirts
smash-stained with blueberries, blackberries,
raspberries. Every fall we'd see them
stumbling along the tracks, leaving town.

Vacationland, the signs said, from here to Lake Erie.
When relatives drove up we took them to see
The Blue Hole, a fenced-in bottomless pit
of water we paid to toss pennies into—
or Prehistoric Forest, where, issued machine guns,
we rode a toy train among life-sized replicas
of brontosaurus and triceratops.

In winter the beanfield behind our house
would freeze over, and I would skate across it

alone late evenings, sometimes tripping
over stubble frozen above the ice.
In spring the fields turned up arrowheads, bones.
Those slow-plowing glaciers left it clean and flat here,
scraping away or pushing underground what was before them.

An Insider's View of the Garden

Maxine Kumin

How can I help but admire the ever perseverant
unquenchable dill
that sways like an unruly crowd at a soccer match
waving its lacy banners
where garlic belongs or slyly invading a hill
of Delicata squash—
how can I help but admire such ardor? I seek it

as bees the flower's core, hummingbirds
the concocted sugar water
that lures them to the feeder in the lilacs.
I praise the springy mane
of untamed tendrils asprawl on chicken wire
that promise to bring forth
peas to overflow a pillowcase.

Some days I adore my coltish broccolis,
the sketchbook beginnings
of their green heads still encauled, incipient trees
sprung from the Pleistocene.
Some days the leeks, that Buckingham Palace patrol
and the quarter-mile of beans
—green, yellow, soy, lima, bush and pole—
demand applause. As do dilatory parsnips,
a ferny dell of tops
regal as celery. Let me laud onion that erupts
slim as a grass stem

then spends the summer inventing its pungent tulip
and the army of brussels sprouts
extending its spoon-shaped leaves over dozens of armpits

that conceal what are now merely thoughts, mere nubbins
needing long ripening.
But let me lament my root-maggot-raddled radishes
my bony and bored red peppers
that drop their lower leaves like dancehall strippers
my cauliflowers that spit
out thimblesize heads in the heat and take beetles to bed.

O children, citizens, my wayward jungly dears
you are all to be celebrated
plucked, transplanted, tilled under, resurrected here
—even the lowly despised
purslane, chickweed, burdock, poke, wild poppies.
For all of you, whether eaten or extirpated
I plan to spend the rest of my life on my knees.

Tahoe in August

Robert Hass

What summer proposes is simply happiness:
heat early in the morning, jays
raucous in the pines. Frank and Ellen have a tennis game
at nine, Bill and Cheryl sleep on the deck
to watch a shower of summer stars. Nick and Sharon
stayed in, sat and talked the dark on,
drinking tea, and Jeanne walked into the meadow
in a white smock to write in her journal
by a grazing horse who seemed to want the company.
Some of them will swim in the afternoon.
Someone will drive to the hardware store to fetch
new latches for the kitchen door. Four o'clock;
the joggers jogging—it is one of them who sees
down the flowering slope the woman with her notebook
in her hand beside the white horse, gesturing, her hair
from a distance the copper color of the hummingbirds
the slant light catches on the slope; the hikers
switchback down the canyon from the waterfall;
the readers are reading, Anna is about to meet Vronsky,
that nice M. Swann is dining in Combray
with the aunts, and Carrie has come to Chicago.
What they want is happiness: someone to love them,
children, a summer by the lake. The woman who sets aside
her book blinks against the fuzzy dark,
re-entering the house. Her daughter drifts downstairs;
out late the night before, she has been napping,
and she's cross. Her mother tells her David telephoned.

"He's such a dear," the mother says, "I think
I made him nervous." The girl tosses her head as the horse
had done in the meadow while Jeanne read it her dream.
"You can call him now, if you want," the mother says,
"I've got to get the chicken started,
I won't listen." "Did I say you would?"
the girl says quickly. The mother who has been slapped
this way before and done the same herself another summer
on a different lake says, "Ouch." The girl shrugs
sulkily. "I'm sorry." Looking down: "Something
about the way you said that pissed me off."
"Hannibal has wandered off," the mother says,
wryness in her voice, she is thinking it is August,
"why don't you see if he's at the Finleys' house
again." The girl says, "God." The mother: "He loves
small children. It's livelier for him there."
The daughter, awake now, flounces out the door,
which slams. It is for all of them the sound of summer.
The mother she looks like stands at the counter snapping beans.

Summer in a Small Town

Linda Gregg

When the men leave me,
they leave me in a beautiful place.
It is always late summer.
When I think of them now,
I think of the place.
And being happy alone afterwards.
This time it's Clinton, New York.
I swim in the public pool
at six when the other people
have gone home.
The sky is gray, the air hot.
I walk back across the mown lawn
loving the smell and the houses
so completely it leaves my heart empty.

The Church of the Backyard

Chris Forhan

Delores wears her celery-colored
swimming suit, the one embellished
with tiny slices of watermelon,
a bite out of each of them.

Assuredly seven, she's eighteen months
and one day older than Ronald, who trips
and sprawls again in the gravel. Last Tuesday
that trick earned a popsicle.

Our newly teenaged sister Vicki
suns herself and paints her toenails green
to match her plastic sandals. Starting today,
she proclaims, we are to call her Victoria.

Mother wears her summer hat: the wide
fried egg that shades her paperback
and wobbles around her ears whenever
she laughs or lifts her head to speak

to father: first one in the pool,
first time out of a business suit
all season, splayed on his inner tube,
circling the deep end, orchid-white.

I've got my Batman outfit on
and, stern-jawed, saunter across the lawn

wearing the others' admiration
lightly. Who would say

through all the little deaths, the separations,
all the long untidy years to come,
each unholy ruckus (the wine glass
smashed against the wall in anger, fists

that pound the steering wheel, bodies
sitting bolt upright in bed with night sweats),
who would say, through all of this,
we're not redeemed by our essential silliness?

Girl Scout Picnic, 1954

June Beisch

The parade began and the Bryant Jr. High School band
     marched through the streets of Minneapolis
wearing white shirts, blue trousers, playing John Philip Sousa

Lance, Jack, Sharon and myself on drums,
     strapped to our knees so we could play,
arms akimbo, drumsticks held high,

drum rolls, paradiddles, rim shots, flams
     while the trumpets groaned and the bystanders
cheered us on in the rain-drenched streets.

The Girl Scouts strutted ahead of us wearing
     their green uniforms, berets and badges
waving the Girl Scout flag, and smiling,

We could do anything after this, we felt,
     twirling our drumsticks between our fingers
Such joy seems unimaginable until I conjure it

Not even Wordsworth's memory of
     a field of daffodils comes close to it
The picnic later at the Minnehaha Falls Park,

then walking home much later in the dark
      still filled with the sounds of it.
To march at thirteen through the streets of Minneapolis

is to ride in triumph through Persepolis.

City of Tonawanda Softball Championship

Sarah Freligh

Two down, two out, two on in the ninth
when Sid Szymanski stands in at catcher,
sorry substitute for Larry whose sure
hands were summoned to a plumbing
emergency by his buzzing pager in the bottom
of the sixth. Still, the usual chatter
Hum baby, hey baby hum hey Sidder Sidder Sidder
though Zack's guys are mentally packing
bats in bags, unlacing shoes in order
to get away—fast—before the Panthers,
arrogant bastards, can gather at home plate
in a love knot of high fives and beer foam
and gloat. Strike two and Sid calls time,
steps out to take a couple of practice cuts
a la Barry Bonds, like him a big man,
all head and chest, and *Siddersiddersidder*
the car keys are out, that's all she wrote
when the pitcher gets cute with a breaking ball,
hanging it a nanosecond too long, time
enough for even fat sad Sid to get around
and give that pill a ride.

Rounding first, already red faced, a crowd
in his throat, Sid wants to believe
it's not the sludge of a million
French fries, but pleasure

more exquisite than the first breast
he touched one winter Sunday
while his dad in the den upstairs
cursed the Packers and Bart Starr, while his mom
chattered on the phone to her friend
Thelma about macaroni casserole
and menstrual cramps, Sid swallowed
hard and bookmarked his place
in *Our Country's History*, the page before
the Marines stormed the hill at Iwo Jima
and turned back the godless Japs, a high tide
clogging his chest as Alice Evans unfastened
the pearl buttons of her white blouse
and presented him with the wrapped gift
of her breasts, now second base and third
and the thicket of hand-slaps all the way
home where Sid hugs the center fielder
hurried and embarrassed the way men do,
oh, the moment, replayed again and again
over Labatt's at Zack's, the first pitcher
delivered by the great Zack himself
rumored to have been the swiftest,
niftiest shortstop on the Cardinal farm
but called to serve in Korea and after that
the closest he got to baseball was standing
next to Ted Williams at a Las Vegas urinal

Tomorrow Zack will make a place
for the trophy between dusty bottles
of Galliano and Kahlua while Sid
will field calls from customers complaining
about rising cable rates and too many queers
on TV, pretty much what he'll be doing
five years from now and ten when his wife

leaves a meatloaf in the freezer and runs off
with Larry the plumber and in twenty years,
when Zack's Bar is bulldozed
to make way for a Wal-Mart,
Sid will slump in a wheelchair
in a hallway littered with old men
mumbling and lost, wrapped
in the soft cloth of memory:
The arc of the white ball, a pearl
in the jewel box of twilight sky.

Baseball

John Updike

It looks easy from a distance,
easy and lazy, even,
until you stand up to the plate
and see the fastball sailing inside,
an inch from your chin,
or circle in the outfield
straining to get a bead
on a small black dot
a city block or more high,
a dark star that could fall
on your head like a leaden meteor.

The grass, the dirt, the deadly hops
between your feet and overeager glove:
football can be learned,
and basketball finessed, but
there is no hiding from baseball
the fact that some are chosen
and some are not—those whose mitts
feel too left-handed,
who are scared at third base
of the pulled line drive,
and at first base are scared
of the shortstop's wild throw
that stretches you out like a gutted deer.

There is nowhere to hide when the ball's
spotlight swivels your way,
and the chatter around you falls still,
and the mothers on the sidelines,
your own among them, hold their breaths,
and you whiff on a terrible pitch
or in the infield achieve
something with the ball so
ridiculous you blush for years.
It's easy to do. Baseball was
invented in America, where beneath
the good cheer and sly jazz the chance
of failure is everybody's right,
beginning with baseball.

The Ordinary

Kirsten Dierking

It's summer, so
the pink gingham shorts,
the red mower, the neat rows
of clean smelling grass
unspooling behind
the sweeping blades.

A dragonfly, black body
big as a finger, will not leave
the mower alone,
loving the sparkle
of scarlet metal,
seeing in even a rusting paint
the shade of a flower.

But I wave him off,
conscious he is
wasting his time,
conscious I am
filling my time
with such small details,
distracting colors,

like pink checks,
like this, then that,
like a dragonfly wing

in the sun reflecting
the color of opals,
like all the hours
we leave behind,
so ordinary,
but not unloved.

The Last Things I'll Remember

Joyce Sutphen

The partly open hay barn door, white frame around the darkness,
the broken board, small enough for a child
to slip through.

Walking in the cornfields in late July, green tassels overhead,
the slap of flat leaves as we pass, silent
and invisible from any road.

Hollyhocks leaning against the stucco house, peonies heavy
as fruit, drooping their deep heads
on the dog house roof.

Lilac bushes between the lawn and the woods,
a tractor shifting from one gear into
the next, the throttle opened,

the smell of cut hay, rain coming across the river,
the drone of the hammer mill,
milk machines at dawn.

A Strange New Cottage in Berkeley

Allen Ginsberg

All afternoon cutting bramble blackberries off a tottering
brown fence
    under a low branch with its rotten old apricots miscellaneous
under the leaves,
    fixing the drip in the intricate gut machinery of a new toilet;
    found a good coffeepot in the vines by the porch, rolled a
big tire out of the scarlet bushes, hid my marijuana;
    wet the flowers, playing the sunlit water each to each,
returning for godly extra drops for the stringbeans and daisies;
    three times walked round the grass and sighed absently:
    my reward, when the garden fed me its plums from the
form of a small tree in the corner,
    an angel thoughtful of my stomach, and my dry and love-
lorn tongue.

So This Is Nebraska

Ted Kooser

The gravel road rides with a slow gallop
over the fields, the telephone lines
streaming behind, its billow of dust
full of the sparks of redwing blackbirds.

On either side, those dear old ladies,
the loosening barns, their little windows
dulled by cataracts of hay and cobwebs
hide broken tractors under their skirts.

So this is Nebraska. A Sunday
afternoon; July. Driving along
with your hand out squeezing the air,
a meadowlark waiting on every post.

Behind a shelterbelt of cedars,
top-deep in hollyhocks, pollen and bees,
a pickup kicks its fenders off
and settles back to read the clouds.

You feel like that; you feel like letting
your tires go flat, like letting the mice
build a nest in your muffler, like being
no more than a truck in the weeds,

clucking with chickens or sticky with honey
or holding a skinny old man in your lap

while he watches the road, waiting
for someone to wave to. You feel like

waving. You feel like stopping the car
and dancing around on the road. You wave
instead and leave your hand out gliding
larklike over the wheat, over the houses.

3

THE PLACE WHERE
WE WERE NAKED

Gradualism

Kenneth Rexroth

We slept naked
On top of the covers and woke
In the chilly dawn and crept
Between the warm sheets and made love
In the morning you said
"It snowed last night on the mountain"
High up on the blue-black diorite
Faint orange streaks of snow
In the ruddy dawn
I said
"It has been snowing for months
All over Canada and Alaska
And Minnesota and Michigan
Right now wet snow is falling
In the morning streets of Chicago
Bit by bit they are making over the world
Even in Mexico even for us"

Belle Isle, 1949

Philip Levine

We stripped in the first warm spring night
and ran down into the Detroit River
to baptize ourselves in the brine
of car parts, dead fish, stolen bicycles,
melted snow. I remember going under
hand in hand with a Polish highschool girl
I'd never seen before, and the cries
our breath made caught at the same time
on the cold, and rising through the layers
of darkness into the final moonless atmosphere
that was this world, the girl breaking
the surface after me and swimming out
on the starless waters towards the lights
of Jefferson Ave. and the stacks
of the old stove factory unwinking.
Turning at last to see no island at all
but a perfect calm dark as far
as there was sight, and then a light
and another riding low out ahead
to bring us home, ore boats maybe, or smokers
walking alone. Back panting
to the gray coarse beach we didn't dare
fall on, the damp piles of clothes,
and dressing side by side in silence
to go back where we came from.

Skinny-Dipping After Work at the Drive-In

Debra Nystrom

No moon; the pickup's headlights stare
across the river from the bluff above, where
fields of sunflower heads turn away,
waiting for dawn. *It's cold*, yelps Amy,
and Brian calls *where are you*
but she screams *no, get away*, so
he and Tommy laugh, dive under for
her legs again. In March I skated over
this same place, past Farm Island, leaving
my track lines in the snow hard to imagine
now, and even then the water must
have moved like this beneath me, erasing
bodies' outlines, as if everything touched
everything all the time.

Jubilee

Gabrielle Calvocoressi

Come down to the water. Bring your snare drum,
your hubcaps, the trash can lid. Bring every
joyful noise you've held at bay so long.
The fish have risen to the surface this early
morning: flounder, shrimp, and every blue crab
this side of Mobile. Bottom feeders? Please.
They shine like your Grandpa Les' Cadillac,
the one you rode in, slow so all the girls
could see. They called to you like katydids.
And the springs in that car sounded like tubas
as you moved up and down. Make a soulful sound
unto the leather and the wheel, praise the man
who had the good sense to build a front seat
like a bed, who knew you'd never buy a car
that big if you only meant to drive it.

Tennis Ball

Donald Hall

I parked by the grave in September, under oaks and birches,
and said hello again, and went walking with Gussie

past markers, roses, and the grave with plastic chickens.
(Somebody loved somebody who loved chickens.)

Gus stopped and stared: A woman's long bare legs
stretched up at the edge of the graveyard, a man's body

heaving between them. Gus considered checking them out,
so I clicked my fingers, as softly as I could, to distract him,

and became the unintending source of *coitus interruptus.*
Walking to the car, I peeked. She was restarting him, her

head riding up and down. It was a fine day, leaves red,
Gus healthy and gay, refusing to give up his tennis ball.

Manhattan

Edward Denham

Up in the sky the lovers lay in bed
Naked, face to face and hip to thigh,
Her leg between his, his arm beneath her head,
Their hands roaming freely, up in the sky.
In the dark, Manhattan lay at their feet,
A blanket of glittering stars thrown down.
Beyond her bare shoulder, 59th Street,
And from her lovely ankle the buses headed uptown.
They came to the city for romance, as people do,
And with each other they scaled the heights
And now, united, they lie at rest, these two,
The bed gently rocking in the sea of lights.
    Where will they go? What happens next? I do not know.
    I am that man waiting at the bus stop far below.

Last Gods

Galway Kinnell

She sits naked on a rock
a few yards out in the water.
He stands on the shore,
also naked, picking blueberries.
She calls. He turns. She opens
her legs showing him her great beauty,
and smiles, a bow of lips
seeming to tie together
the ends of the earth.
Splashing her image
to pieces, he wades out
and stands before her, sunk
to the anklebones in leaf-mush
and bottom-slime—the intimacy
of the geographical. He puts
a berry in its shirt
of mist into her mouth.
She swallows it. He puts in another.
She swallows it. Over the lake
two swallows whim, juke, jink,
and when one snatches
an insect they both whirl up
and exult. He is swollen
not with ichor but with blood.
She takes him and talks him
more swollen. He kneels, opens
the dark, vertical smile

linking heaven with the underearth
and murmurs her smoothest flesh more smooth.
On top of the rock they join.
Somewhere a frog moans, a crow screams.
The hair of their bodies
startles up. They cry
in the tongue of the last gods,
who refused to go,
chose death, and shuddered
in joy and shattered in pieces,
bequeathing their cries
into the human mouth. Now in the lake
two faces float, looking up
at a great maternal pine whose branches
open out in all directions
explaining everything.

Breaking Silence—For My Son

Patricia Fargnoli

The night you were conceived
your father drove up Avon Mountain
and into the roadside rest
that looked over the little city,
its handful of scattered sparks.
I was eighteen and thin then
but the front seat of the 1956 Dodge
seemed cramped and dark,
the new diamond, I hadn't known
how to refuse, trapping flecks of light.
Even then the blackness was thick
as a muck you could swim through.
Your father pushed me down
on the scratchy seat, not roughly
but as if staking a claim,
and his face rose like
a thin-shadowed moon above me.
My legs ached in those peculiar angles,
my head bumped against the door.
I know you want me to say I loved him
but I wanted only to belong—to anyone.
So I let it happen,
the way I let all of it happen—
the marriage, his drinking, the rage.
This is not to say I loved you any less—
only I was young and didn't know yet
we can choose our lives.

It was dark in the car.
Such weight and pressure,
the wet earthy smell of night,
a slickness like glue.
And in a distant inviolate place,
as though it had nothing at all
to do with him, you were a spark
in silence catching.

Late

Jim Harrison

What pleasure there is in sitting up on the sofa late at night smoking cigarettes, having a small last drink and petting the dogs, reading Virgil's sublime *Georgics*, seeing a girl's bare bottom on TV that you will likely never see again in what they call real life, remembering all the details of when you were captured by the indians at age seven. They gave you time off for good behavior but never truly let you go back to your real world where cars go two ways on the same streets. The doctors will say it's bad for an old man to stay up late petting his lovely dogs. Meanwhile I look up from Virgil's farms of ancient Rome and see two women making love in a field of wildflowers. I'm not jealous of their real passion trapped as they are within a television set just as my doctors are trapped within their exhausting days and big incomes that have to be spent. Lighting a last cigarette and sipping my vodka I examine the faces of the sleeping dogs beside me, the improbable mystery of their existence, the short lives they live with an intensity unbearable to us. I have turned to them for their ancient language not my own, being quite willing to give up my language that so easily forgets the world outside itself.

4

CITY LIFE

New York Notes

Harvey Shapiro

1.

Caught on a side street
in heavy traffic, I said
to the cabbie, I should
have walked. He replied,
I should have been a doctor.

2.

When can I get on the 11:33
I ask the guy in the information booth
at the Atlantic Avenue Station.
When they open the doors, he says.
I am home among my people.

Mannahatta

Walt Whitman

I was asking for something specific and perfect for my city,
Whereupon lo! upsprang the aboriginal name.
Now I see what there is in a name, a word, liquid, sane, unruly,
    musical, self-sufficient,
I see that the word of my city is that word from of old,
Because I see that word nested in nests of water-bays, superb,
Rich, hemm'd thick all around with sailships and steamships, an
    island sixteen miles long, solid-founded,
Numberless crowded streets, high growths of iron, slender, strong,
    light, splendidly uprising toward clear skies,
Tides swift and ample, well-loved by me, toward sundown,
The flowing sea-currents, the little islands, larger adjoining islands,
    the heights, the villas,
The countless masts, the white shore-steamers, the lighters, the
    ferry-boats, the black sea-steamers well-model'd,
The down-town streets, the jobbers' houses of business, the houses
    of business of the ship-merchants and money-brokers, the
    river-streets,
Immigrants arriving, fifteen or twenty thousand in a week,
The carts hauling goods, the manly race of drivers of horses, the
    brown-faced sailors,
The summer air, the bright sun shining, and the sailing clouds
    aloft,
The winter snows, the sleigh-bells, the broken ice in the river,
    passing along up or down with the flood-tide or ebb-tide,

The mechanics of the city, the masters, well-form'd, beautiful-
    faced, looking you straight in the eyes,
Trottoirs throng'd, vehicles, Broadway, the women, the shops and
    shows,
A million people—manners free and superb—open voices—
    hospitality—the most courageous and friendly young men,
City of hurried and sparkling waters! city of spires and masts!
City nested in bays! my city!

New York

Edward Field

I live in a beautiful place, a city
people claim to be astonished
when you say you live there.
They talk of junkies, muggings, dirt, and noise,
missing the point completely.
I tell them where they live it is hell,
a land of frozen people.
They never think of people.

Home, I am astonished by this environment
that is also a form of nature
like those paradises of trees and grass,
but this is a people paradise,
where we are the creatures mostly,
though thank God for dogs, cats, sparrows, and roaches.
This vertical place is no more an accident
than the Himalayas are.
The city needs all those tall buildings
to contain the tremendous energy here.
The landscape is in a state of balance.
We do God's will whether we know it or not:
where I live the streets end in a river of sunlight.

Nowhere else in the country do people
show just what they feel—
we don't put on any act.

Look at the way New Yorkers
walk down the street. It says,
I don't care. What nerve,
to dare to live their dreams, or nightmares,
and no one bothers to look.

True, you have to be an expert to live here.
Part of the trick is not to go anywhere, lounge about,
go slowly in the midst of the rush for novelty.
Anyway, besides the eats the big event here
is the streets, which are full of love—
we hug and kiss a lot. You can't say that
for anywhere else around. For some
it's a carnival of sex—
there's all the opportunity in the world.
For me it is no different:
out walking, my soul seeks its food.
It knows what it wants.
Instantly it recognizes its mate, our eyes meet,
and our beings exchange a vital energy,
the universe goes on Charge,
and we pass by without holding.

Staying at Ed's Place

May Swenson

I like being in your apartment, and not disturbing
        anything.
As in the woods I wouldn't want to move a tree,
or change the play of sun and shadow on the ground.

The yellow kitchen stool belongs right there
against white plaster. I haven't used your purple towel
because I like the accidental cleft of shade you left in it.

At your small six-sided table, covered with mysterious
dents in the wood like a dartboard, I drink my coffee
from your brown mug. I look into the clearing

of your high front room, where sunlight slopes
        through bare
window squares. Your Afghanistan hammock,
        a man-sized cocoon
slung from wall to wall, your narrow desk and
        typewriter

are the only furniture. Each morning your light from
        the east
douses me where, with folded legs, I sit in your
        meadow,
a casual spread of brilliant carpets. Like a cat or dog

I take a roll, then, stretched out flat
in the center of color and pattern, I listen
to the remote growl of trucks over cobbles on Bethune
      Street below.

When I open my eyes I discover the peaceful blank
of the ceiling. Its old paint-layered surface is
      moonwhite
and trackless, like the Sea—of Tranquillity.

My Daughters in New York

James Reiss

What streets, what taxis transport them
over bridges & speed bumps—my daughters swift

in pursuit of union? What suitors amuse them, what mazes
of avenues tilt & confuse them as pleasure, that pinball

goes bouncing off light posts & lands in a pothole,
only to pop up & roll in the gutter? What footloose new

freedoms allow them to plow through all stop signs,
careening at corners, hell-bent for the road to blaze straight?

It's 10 P.M. in the boonies. My children, I'm thinking
you're thinking your children are waiting

for you to conceive them while you're in a snarl
with my sons-in-law-to-be who want also to be

amazing explorers beguiled by these reckless night rides
that may God willing give way to ten thousand good mornings!

At the Algonquin

Howard Moss

He sat at the Algonquin, smoking a cigar.
A coffin of a clock bonged out the time.
She was ten minutes late. But in that time,
He puffed the blue eternity of his cigar.

Did she love him still? His youth was gone.
Humiliation's toad, with its blank stares
Squatted on his conscience. When they went upstairs,
Some version of them both would soon be gone.

Before that, though, drinks, dinner, and a play—
The whole demanding, dull expense account
You paid these days for things of no account.
Whatever love may be, it's not child's play.

Slowly she walked toward him. God, we are
Unnatural animals! The scent of roses
Filled the room above the carpet's roses,
And, getting up, he said, "Ah, *there* you are!"

The Last Bohemians

Edward Field

For Rosetta Reitz

We meet in a cheap diner and I think, God,
the continuity, I mean, imagine
our still being here together
from the old days of the Village
when you had the bookshop on Greenwich Avenue
and Jimmy Baldwin and Jimmy Merrill used to drop in.

Toying with your gooey chicken, you remind me
how disappointed I was with you for moving
to Eighth Street and adding gifts and art cards,
but little magazines, you explain, couldn't pay the rent.
Don't apologize, I want to say, it was forty years ago!

Neither of us, without clinging to our old apartments,
could pay Village rents nowadays,
where nobody comes "to be an artist" anymore.
Living marginally still, we are shabby as ever,
though shabby was attractive on us once—those years
when the latest Williams or Stevens or Moore was sold
in maybe five bookstores, and the Horton
biography of Hart Crane an impossible find.
Continuity! We're still talking of our problems
with writing, finding a publisher,
as though that was the most important thing in the world.
Sweetheart, we are as out of it as old lefties.

Someone came into my apartment recently and exclaimed,
"Why, it's bohemian!" as if she had discovered
the last of a near-extinct breed.
Lady, I wanted to protest,
I don't have clamshell ashtrays,
or Chianti bottles encrusted with candle wax,
or Wilhelm Reich, Henry Miller, and D. H. Lawrence,
much less Kahlil Gibran and Havelock Ellis,
on my bricks-and-boards bookshelves!
But it's not just the Salvation Army junk she saw
or the mattress and pillows on the floor.
My living style represented for her
the aesthetic of an earlier generation,
the economics, even, of a time,
our time, Rosetta, before she was born.

The youth still come weekends, though not to
"see a drag show,"
or "bull daggers fighting in the gutters,"
or to "pick up a queer or artist's model."
But there is something expectant in them
for something supposed to be here, once called,
(shiver) bohemian. Now it's I who shiver
as I pass them, fearing their rage against
an old guy with the sad face of a loser.
Daytime, it's safer, with couples in from the suburbs
browsing the antique shops.
I find it all so boring, but am stuck here,
a ghost in a haunted house.

At a movie about a war criminal whose American
lawyer daughter blindly defends him, blasted by the critics

because it is serious and has a message,
the audience is full of old Villagers, drawn to see it
because it's serious and has a message,
the women, no longer in dirndls and sandals,
but with something telltale about the handcrafted jewelry,
the men not in berets, but the kind that would wear them,
couples for whom being young meant being radical,
meant free love. Anyway,
something about them says Villager,
maybe the remnants of intellect, idealism,
which has begun to look odd on American faces.

Nowadays, there's nothing radical left, certainly not
in the Village, no Left Bank to flee to, no justification
for artistic poverty, nothing for the young to believe in,
except their careers and the fun of flaunting
their youth and freaky hairstyles in trendy enclaves.

Leftovers from the old Village, we spot each other
drifting through the ghostly
high-rental picturesque streets, ears echoing
with typewriters clacking and scales and arpeggios
heard no more, and meet fugitive in coffee shops,
partly out of friendship, but also, as we get shabbier and rarer,
from a sense of continuity like, hey, we're historic!
and an appreciation, even if we never quite got there,
of what our generation set out to do.

At the Museum of Modern Art

May Swenson

At the Museum of Modern Art you can sit in the lobby
on the foam-rubber couch; you can rest and smoke,
and view whatever the revolving doors express.
You don't have to go into the galleries at all.

In this arena the exhibits are free and have all
the surprises of art—besides something extra:
sensory restlessness, the play of alternation,
expectation in an incessant spray

thrown from heads, hands, the tendons of ankles.
The shifts and strollings of feet
engender compositions on the shining tiles,
and glide together and pose gambits,

gestures of design, that scatter, rearrange,
trickle into lines, and turn clicking through a wicket
into rooms where caged colors blotch the walls.
You don't have to go to the movie downstairs

to sit on red plush in the snow and fog
of old-fashioned silence. You can see contemporary
Garbos and Chaplins go by right here.
And there's a mesmeric experimental film

constantly reflected on the flat side of the wide
steel-plate pillar opposite the crenellated window.

Non-objective taxis surging west, on Fifty-third,
liquefy in slippery yellows, dusky crimsons,

pearly mauves—an accelerated sunset, a roiled
surf, or cloud-curls undulating—their tubular ribbons
elongations of the coils of light itself
(engine of color) and motion (motor of form).

Bridal Shower

George Bilgere

Perhaps, in a distant café,
four or five people are talking
with the four or five people
who are chatting on their cell phones this morning
in my favorite café.

And perhaps someone there,
someone like me, is watching them as they frown,
or smile, or shrug
at their invisible friends or lovers,
jabbing the air for emphasis.

And, like me, he misses the old days,
when talking to yourself
meant you were crazy,
back when being crazy was a big deal,
not just an acronym
or something you could take a pill for.

I liked it
when people who were talking to themselves
might actually have been talking to God
or an angel.
You respected people like that.

You didn't want to kill them,
as I want to kill the woman at the next table

with the little blue light on her ear
who has been telling the emptiness in front of her
about her daughter's bridal shower
in astonishing detail
for the past thirty minutes.

O person like me,
phoneless in your distant café,
I wish we could meet to discuss this,
and perhaps you would help me
murder this woman on her cell phone,

after which we could have a cup of coffee,
maybe a bagel, and talk to each other,
face to face.

What the Dark-Eyed Angel Knows

Eleanor Lerman

A man is begging on his knees in the subway. Six-thirty
in the morning and already we are being presented with
moral choices as we rocket along the old rails, through the
old tunnels between Queens and Manhattan. Soon angels
will come crashing through the ceiling, wailing in the voices
of the castrati: *Won't you give this pauper bread or money?*
And a monster hurricane is coming: we all heard about it
on the radio at dawn. By nightfall, drowned hogs will be
floating like poisoned soap bubbles on the tributaries
of every Southern river. Children will be orphaned and
the infrastructure of whole cities will be overturned. No one
on the East Coast will be able to make a phone call and we
will be boiling our water for days. And of course there are
the serial killers. And the Crips and the Bloods. And the
arguments about bilingual education. And the fact that all
the clothing made by slave labor overseas is not only the
product of an evil system but maybe worse, never even fits

so why is it that all I can think of (and will think of through
the torrential rains to come and the howling night) is
you, sighing so deeply in the darkness, you and the smell
of you and the windswept curve of your cheek? If this
train ever stops, I will ask that dark-eyed angel, the one
who hasn't spoken yet. He looks like he might know

Riding the "A"

May Swenson

I ride
the "A" train
and feel
like a ball-
bearing in a roller skate.
I have on a gray
rain-
coat. The hollow
of the car
is gray.
My face
a negative in the slate
window,
I sit
in a lit
corridor that races
through a dark
one. Strok-
ing steel,
what a smooth rasp—it feels
like the newest of knives
slicing
along
a long
black crusty loaf
from West 4th to 168th.
Wheels

and rails
in their prime
collide,
make love in a glide
of slickness
and friction.
It is an elation
I wish to pro-
long.
The station
is reached
too soon.

Goodbye, New York

(song from the wrong side of the Hudson)

Deborah Garrison

You were the big fat city we called hometown
You were the lyrics I sang but never wrote down

You were the lively graves by the highway in Queens
the bodega where I bought black beans

stacks of the *Times* we never read
nights we never went to bed

the radio jazz, the doughnut cart
the dogs off their leashes in Tompkins Square Park

You were the tiny brass mailbox key
the joy of "us" and the sorrow of "me"

You were the balcony bar in Grand Central Station
the blunt commuters and their destination

the post-wedding blintzes at 4 A.M.
and the pregnant waitress we never saw again

You were the pickles, you were the jar
You were the prizefight we watched in a bar

the sloppy kiss in the basement at Nell's
the occasional truth that the fortune cookie tells

Sinatra still swinging at Radio City
You were ugly and gorgeous but never pretty

always the question, never the answer
the difficult poet, the aging dancer

the call I made from a corner phone
to a friend in need, who wasn't at home

the fireworks we watched from a tenement roof
the brash allegations and the lack of any proof

my skyline, my byline, my buzzer and door
now you're the dream we lived before

For Bartleby

Malena Mörling

Tonight I wonder where the man is
    who used to stand just inside the doors
of the Lexington Avenue entrance to Grand Central Station.

The full moon is rising. Around the earth, meteors move
    through space. Every day for over a year
I walked by him early in the morning

    and at the end of the day he still
stood in the same position, arms down
    his sides, looking straight ahead

at thousands of people walking
    without colliding in all directions at once,
everybody trying to get to a different place.

Moondog

Susan Donnelly

He just stood there,
at the corner of 43rd Street
and Sixth Avenue,
nearly seven feet tall,
dressed as a Viking.
Everyone, it seemed,
in New York in the '60s
knew Moondog. They said
he'd been a stockbroker,
from a rich family.
They said he was blind.

I was writing a novel that year,
but didn't know how,
and falling in love,
and everything moved so fast,
but the Viking was motionless.
I know he wrote songs,
but I never heard any.
He just stared outward.
I'd wake up, write myself dizzy,
then go walking, fast,
through the streets.

One day, a stranger
stopped me: JFK had been shot!
This was in midtown. The bells

of St. Patrick's began tolling
and I joined all the others
going up the cathedral steps.
I'd seen the President
just last month—young,
glinting like silver,
in a limousine going up Madison
to the Hotel Carlyle.
He waved to all of us
and we waved back, cheering . . .

Or are these tears
for the broken love,
the unreadable novel?
Anyway, the years.

Home By Now

Meg Kearney

New Hampshire air curls my hair like a child's
hand curls around a finger. "Children?" No,
we tell the realtor, but maybe a dog or two.
They'll bark at the mail car (Margaret's
Chevy Supreme) and chase the occasional
moose here in this place where doors are left
unlocked and it's Code Green from sun-up,
meaning go ahead and feel relieved—
the terrorists are back where you left them
on East 20th Street and Avenue C. In New York
we stocked our emergency packs with whistles
and duct tape. In New England, precautions take
a milder hue: don't say "pig" on a lobster boat
or paint the hull blue. Your friends in the city
say they'll miss but don't blame you—they
still cringe each time a plane's overhead,
one ear cocked for the other shoe.

Black Umbrellas

Rick Agran

On a rainy day in Seattle stumble into any coffee shop
and look wounded by the rain.

Say *Last time I was in I left my black umbrella here.*
A waitress in a blue beret will pull a black umbrella

from behind the counter and surrender it to you
like a sword at your knighting.

Unlike New Englanders, she'll never ask you
to describe it, never ask what day you came in,

she's intimate with rain and its appointments.
Look positively reunited with this black umbrella

and proceed to Belltown and Pike Place.
Sip cappuccino at the Cowgirl Luncheonette on First Ave.

Visit Buster selling tin salmon silhouettes
undulant in the wind, nosing ever into the oncoming,

meandering watery worlds, like you and the black umbrella,
the one you will lose on purpose at the day's end

so you can go the way you came
into the world, wet looking.

A New Lifestyle

James Tate

People in this town drink too much
coffee. They're jumpy all the time. You
see them drinking out of their big plastic
mugs while they're driving. They cut in
front of you, they steal your parking places.
Teenagers in the cemeteries knocking over
tombstones are slurping café au lait.
Recycling men hanging onto their trucks are
sipping espresso. Dogcatchers running down
the street with their nets are savoring
their cups of mocha java. The holdup man
entering a convenience store first pours
himself a nice warm cup of coffee. Down
the funeral parlor driveway a boy on a
skateboard is spilling his. They're so
serious about their coffee, it's all they
can think about, nothing else matters.
Everyone's wide awake but looks incredibly
tired.

Motor City Tirade

Dawn McDuffie

Send us your homeless, your crazy.
The lady who wears a wedding veil
every day with her fox stole and twenty necklaces—
better she lives in the city; she would be locked up
after one day on the clean streets
of Bloomfield Hills.
Hookers belong in the city
just like wastewater sent in from the county
in exchange for clean water pumped back
for comfortable lives.
Whole rivers flow under the pavements,
constrained by tiles, carrying no light
but still making a path to the Great Lakes.
And hidden children in ghetto schools
breathe burning garbage,
roach droppings and asbestos dust,
and flunk out when they miss
too many days.
They don't visit the shiny casino
that displaced the local pool.
Now we must host the happy gambler.
Nothing as perfect as those casino streets
edged with pots of pink geraniums.
Oh, it can be so pleasant here and also
near the mayor's house where the four-foot
snowfall is promptly whisked away

while the rest of us pray the electricity
won't give out. Aging circuits
keep the lights flickering. I watch them
up and down the street from my house,
wires popping and writhing
when the load just gets too heavy.

Beale Street Blues

W. C. Handy

I've seen the lights of gay Broadway,
Old Market Street down by the Frisco Bay,
I've strolled the Prado, I've gambled on the Bourse
The seven wonders of the world I've seen
And many are the places I have been.

Take my advice folks and see Beale Street first.

You'll see pretty Browns in beautiful gowns,
You'll see tailor-mades and hand-me-downs
You'll meet honest men and pickpockets skilled,
You'll find that bus'ness never closes till somebody gets killed.

You'll see Hog-Nose rest'rants and Chitlin' Cafés,
You'll see Jugs that tell of by-gone days,
And places, once places, now just a sham,
You'll see Golden Balls enough to pave the New Jerusalem.

If Beale Street could talk,
If Beale Street could talk,
Married men would have to take their beds and walk,
Except one or two, who never drink booze,
And the blind man on the corner who sings the Beale Street Blues.

I'd rather be here than any place I know,
I'd rather be here than any place I know

It's goin' to take the Sargent
For to make me go,

Goin' to the river,
Maybe, bye and bye,
Goin' to the river, and there's a reason why,
Because the river's wet,
And Beale Street's done gone dry.

Motown, Arsenal of Democracy

Marge Piercy

Fog used to bloom off the distant river
turning our streets strange, elongating
sounds and muffling others. The crack
of a gunshot softened.

The sky at night was a dull red:
a bonfire built of old creosote soaked
logs by the railroad tracks. A red
almost pink painted by factories—

that never stopped their roar
like traffic in canyons of New York.
But stop they did and fell down
ending dangerous jobs that paid.

We believed in our unions like some
trust in their priests. We believed
in Friday paychecks sure as
winter's ice curb-to-curb

where older boys could play
hockey dodging cars—wooden
pucks, sticks cracking wood
on wood. A man came home

with a new car and other men
would collect around it like ants

in sugar. Women clumped for showers—
wedding and baby—wakes, funerals

care for the man brought home
with a hole ripped in him, children
coughing. We all coughed in Detroit.
We woke at dawn to my father's hack.

That world is gone as a tableau
of wagon trains. Expressways carved
neighborhoods to shreds. Rich men
moved jobs south, then overseas.

Only the old anger lives there
bubbling up like chemicals dumped
seething now into the water
building now into the bones.

Fishing on the Susquehanna in July

Billy Collins

I have never been fishing on the Susquehanna
or on any river for that matter
to be perfectly honest.

Not in July or any month
have I had the pleasure—if it is a pleasure—
of fishing on the Susquehanna.

I am more likely to be found
in a quiet room like this one—
a painting of a woman on the wall,

a bowl of tangerines on the table—
trying to manufacture the sensation
of fishing on the Susquehanna.

There is little doubt
that others have been fishing
on the Susquehanna,

rowing upstream in a wooden boat,
sliding the oars under the water
then raising them to drip in the light.

But the nearest I have ever come to
fishing on the Susquehanna
was one afternoon in a museum in Philadelphia,

when I balanced a little egg of time
in front of a painting
in which that river curled around a bend

under a blue cloud-ruffled sky,
dense trees along the banks,
and a fellow with a red bandana

sitting in a small, green
flat-bottom boat
holding the thin whip of a pole.

That is something I am unlikely
ever to do, I remember
saying to myself and the person next to me.

Then I blinked and moved on
to other American scenes
of haystacks, water whitening over rocks,

even one of a brown hare
who seemed so wired with alertness
I imagined him springing right out of the frame.

Pershing Square, Los Angeles, 1939

Charles Bukowski

One orator proving there was a God
and another proving that there wasn't.
and the crazy lady with the white and yellow
hair with the big dirty blue ribbon,
the white-striped dress, the tennis shoes,
the bare dirty ankles and the big dog
with the matted hardened fur.
and there was the guitar player and
the drum player and the flute player
all about, the winos sleeping on
the lawn
and all the while the war was rushing
toward us
but somehow nobody argued about the
war
or at least I never heard them.

in the late afternoon I would go into
one of the bars on 6th street.
I was 19 but I looked 30.
I ordered scotch-and-water.
I sat in a booth and nobody bothered
me
as the war rushed toward us.
as the afternoon dipped into evening
I refused to pay for my drinks.
and demanded more.

"Give me another drink or I'll
rip this place up!"
"All right," they told me, "one
more but it's the last and don't
come back, please."
I liked being young and mean.
the world didn't make any sense
to me.

as the night darkened I'd go back
to Pershing Square
and sit on the benches and watch
and listen to the
people.
the winos on the lawn passed bottles
of muscatel and port about
as the war rushed toward
us.

I wasn't interested in the war.
I didn't have anything, I didn't want
anything.
I had my half pint of whiskey and I
nipped at it, rolled cigarettes
and waited.
I'd read half the books in the library
and had spit them out.

the war rushed toward us.
the guitar player played his guitar.
the drummer beat his drums.
and the flute player played that thing
and it rushed toward us,
the air was clear and cool.

the stars seemed just a thousand feet
away above us
and you could see the red burning tips of
cigarettes
and there were people coughing and
laughing and swearing,
and some babbled and some prayed
and many just sat there doing
nothing,
there was nothing to do,
it was 1939 and it would never be
1939 again
in Los Angeles or any place
else
and I was young and mean and
lean
and I would never be that way
again
as it rushed toward
us.

LA

Terry Stevenson

We forget
where priests buried the Indians
and where the Valley got its water.
We debate how close
to a fault line we can build the subway.
The stress shows, LA falls apart.
I'm beginning to crack too.
Out spills my love child,
my marriages and divorces,
three ex-wives and my lover,
the mother of my daughter,
now a teenager,
all legs and attitude,
out comes the Zoot Suit Riots, flat-brimmed hats
on that June night in '43
when the GIs went crazy,
beating up every *pachuco* they could find,
Belushi at the Chateau Marmont,
dancing in the penthouse
with the ghosts of Flynn and Harlow,
the Black Dahlia, Benedict Canyon, and Brentwood,
a history of sharp knives,
Chavez Ravine, families evicted
for O'Malley's Dodgers,
my father, murdered in Hollywood,
the Chinese Massacre of 1871,
the tongs pissed off the locals,

19 Chinese killed, 15 of them
hanged over Calle de los Negros,
Japanese-Americans living
in Santa Anita horse stalls
waiting for the trip to Manzanar,
the police retreat from Florence and Normandie,
letting the neighborhood burn.

Interiors

Stephen Dunn

In New Orleans, a Bed and Breakfast in a seamy part of
town. Dentist's chair the seat of honor in the living room.
Dark, the drapes closed, a lamp's three-way bulb clicked just
once. I'm inside someone's version of inside. All the guests
looking like they belong. Muffled hilarity coming from one
of the other rooms. Paintings everywhere, on the walls, the
floor. Painted by the proprietress who, on the side, reads the
Tarot. In her long black gown she doesn't mind telling me
things look rather dismal. Something about the Queen of
Swords and the Hanged Man. I wake early the next morning
for a flight. 5 A.M. She's sitting in the dentist's chair, reading a
book about the end of the century. Says a man like me needs
a proper breakfast. Wants to know everything I dreamed.
This, I tell her, I think I dreamed this.

Reading, PA

John Updike

Munificence of textiles, coal and steel
set a surreal pagoda on Mt. Penn
and filled the Schuylkill Valley with a grid
of tight-packed workingmen's rowhouses. When
the jobs moved south and malls came in, downtown—
five first-run movie houses! Pomeroy's
Department Store! soft pretzels! Santa Claus!—
went hollow, but for some Hispanic boys.

The child I once was marveled, *City life!*—
trolleys with bright cane seats, a bustling race
of women in perms and hats, and portly men
in vests and pocket watches, a *populace*.
Now where they shopped and movies showed there is
blank blue glass: banks and welfare offices.

The Elm City

Reed Whittemore

The hard, yellow, reversible, wicker seats
Sit in my mind's warm eye, varnished row on row,
In the old yellow childhood trolley
At the end of the line at Cliff Street, where the conductor
Swings the big wooden knob on the tall control box,
Clangs the dishpan bell, and we wander off

To tiptoe on stones and look up at bones in cases
In the cold old stone and bone of the Peabody Museum,
Where the dinosaur and the mastodon stare us down,
And the Esquimaux and the Indians stare us down

In New Haven,
The Elm City.

I left that town long ago for war and folly.
Phylogeny rolled to a stop at the old Peabody.
I still hear the dishpan bell of the yellow trolley.

Profile of the Night Heron

Anne Pierson Wiese

In the Brooklyn Botanic Garden the night
heron is on his branch of his tree, blue
moon curve of his body riding low
above the pond, leaves dipping into water
beneath him, green and loose as fingers.
On the far shore, the ibis is where
I left him last time, a black cypher
on his rock. These birds, they go to the right
place every day until they die.

There are people like that in the city,
with signature hats or empty attaché cases,
expressions of private absorption fending
off comment, who attach to physical
locations—a storefront, a stoop, a corner,
a bench—and appear there daily as if for a job.
They negotiate themselves into the pattern
of place, perhaps wiping windows, badly,
for a few bucks, clearing the stoop of take-out
menus every morning, collecting the trash
at the base of the WALK/DON'T WALK sign
and depositing it in the garbage can.

Even when surfaces change, when the Mom & Pop
store becomes a coffee bar, when the park

benches are replaced with dainty chairs and a pebble
border, they stay, noticing what will never change:
the heartprick of longitude and latitude
to home in on, the conviction that life
depends, every day, on what outlasts you.

Retired Ballerinas, Central Park West

Lawrence Ferlinghetti

Retired ballerinas on winter afternoons
   walking their dogs
   in Central Park West
   (or their cats on leashes—
   the cats themselves old highwire artists)
The ballerinas
   leap and pirouette
   through Columbus Circle
   while winos on park benches
   (laid back like drunken Goudonovs)
   hear the taxis trumpet together
   like horsemen of the apocalypse
   in the dusk of the gods
It is the final witching hour
   when swains are full of swan songs
   And all return through the dark dusk
   to their bright cells
   in glass highrises
   or sit down to oval cigarettes and cakes
   in the Russian Tea Room
   or climb four flights to back rooms
   in Westside brownstones
   where faded playbill photos
   fall peeling from their frames
   like last year's autumn leaves

The Old Neighbors

Katha Pollitt

The weather's turned, and the old neighbors creep out
from their crammed rooms to blink in the sun, as if
surprised to find they've lived through another winter.
Though steam heat's left them pale and shrunken
like old root vegetables,
Mr. and Mrs. Tozzi are already
hard at work on their front-yard mini-Sicily:
a Virgin Mary birdbath, a thicket of roses,
and the only outdoor aloes in Manhattan.
It's the old immigrant story,
the beautiful babies
grown up into foreigners. Nothing's
turned out the way they planned
as sweethearts in the sinks of Palermo. Still,
each waves a dirt-caked hand
in geriatric fellowship with Stanley,
the former tattoo king of the Merchant Marine,
turning the corner with his shaggy collie,
who's hardly three but trots
arthritically in sympathy. It's only
the young who ask if life's worth living, not
Mrs. Sansanowitz, who for the last hour
has been inching her way down the sidewalk,
lifting and placing
her new aluminum walker as carefully
as a spider testing its web. On days like these,

I stand for a long time
under the wild gnarled root of the ancient wisteria,
dry twigs that in a week
will manage a feeble shower of purple blossom,
and I believe it: this is all there is,
all history's brought us here to our only life
to find, if anywhere,
our hanging gardens and our street of gold:
cracked stoops, geraniums, fire escapes, these old
stragglers basking in their bit of sun.

5

2 X 2 X 2

Once I Pass'd through a Populous City

Walt Whitman

Once I pass'd through a populous city imprinting my brain
    for future use with its shows, architecture, customs, traditions,
Yet now of all that city I remember only a woman I casually met
    there who detain'd me for love of me,
Day by day and night by night we were together—all else
    has long been forgotten by me,
I remember I say only that woman who passionately clung to me,
Again we wander, we love, we separate again,
Again she holds me by the hand, I must not go,
I see her close beside me with silent lips sad and tremulous.

Gate C22

Ellen Bass

At gate C22 in the Portland airport
a man in a broad-band leather hat kissed
a woman arriving from Orange County.
They kissed and kissed and kissed. Long after
the other passengers clicked the handles of their carry-ons
and wheeled briskly toward short-term parking,
the couple stood there, arms wrapped around each other
like he'd just staggered off the boat at Ellis Island,
like she'd been released at last from ICU, snapped
out of a coma, survived bone cancer, made it down
from Annapurna in only the clothes she was wearing.

Neither of them was young. His beard was gray.
She carried a few extra pounds you could imagine
her saying she had to lose. But they kissed lavish
kisses like the ocean in the early morning,
the way it gathers and swells, sucking
each rock under, swallowing it
again and again. We were all watching—
passengers waiting for the delayed flight
to San Jose, the stewardesses, the pilots,
the aproned woman icing Cinnabons, the man selling
sunglasses. We couldn't look away. We could
taste the kisses crushed in our mouths.

But the best part was his face. When he drew back
and looked at her, his smile soft with wonder, almost

as though he were a mother still open from giving birth,
as your mother must have looked at you, no matter
what happened after—if she beat you or left you or
you're lonely now—you once lay there, the vernix
not yet wiped off, and someone gazed at you
as if you were the first sunrise seen from the Earth.
The whole wing of the airport hushed,
all of us trying to slip into that woman's middle-aged body,
her plaid Bermuda shorts, sleeveless blouse, glasses,
little gold hoop earrings, tilting our heads up.

Escape from Paradise, Iowa

Kathryn Kysar

We are afraid of nothing.
At the diner,
you order a burger,
a grilled cheese for me.
We tell bad jokes,
pour salt on the table.
The waitress glares at us,
our clothes too tight,
my lipstick too red
for this small town.

This is the summer
of anger and beer.
We know everything:
how each blade of grass turns in the wind,
why the sunlight glints off the pool,
the shining of streetlights on black pavement,
the darkness of the lake at night.

At the bar
you say I am as Nordic
as blonde hair, these big bones
under the sheet of my skin
a frame for your thoughts.
I am the only one smoking.
My breath peels into the air like waves.

We have nothing in this town:
a beat-up Mustang,
a few songs on the jukebox,
the torn cover of a book you never read.
When we get in the car,
you pass me another beer.

We are scared of these random roads,
the small towns passing,
the gas tank nearly empty.
My head on your shoulder,
the eight track stuck again,
we're gonna drive this dirt road
all the way to Kansas City.

Every Day, the Pregnant Teenagers

Cortney Davis

assemble at my desk, backpacks
jingling, beepers on their belts like hand grenades,
and inside, their babies
swirl like multicolored pinwheels in a hurricane.

The girls raise too-big smocks, show me
the stretched-tight skin
from under which a foot or hand thumps,
knocks, makes the belly wobble.

A girl strokes her invisible child,
recites all possible names, as if a name
might carry laundry down the street or fix
a Chevrolet. I measure months

with a paper tape, maneuver the cold stethoscope
that lifts a fetal heart-*swoosh* into air.
Then, shirts billowing like parachutes,
the girls fly to Filene's where infant shoes,

on sale, have neon strobes and satin bows—*oh,*
Renee, Shalika, Blanca, Marie,
the places you'll go, the places you'll go!

A Girl in Milwaukee and a Girl in Brooklyn

Matt Cook

My wife is talking on the phone in Milwaukee
To her girlfriend in Brooklyn.
But, in the middle of all that, my wife has to go pee.
And it turns out that the girl in Brooklyn,
At the very same time, also has to go pee.
So they discuss this for a moment,
And they're both very intelligent people.
They decide to set their phones down and go to the bathroom
(This was back when people set their phones down).
So they do this, and now we have a live telephone line open
Between Milwaukee and Brooklyn
With no one speaking through it for about two minutes as
A girl in Milwaukee and a girl in Brooklyn go to the bathroom.

The Day I Made My Father Proud

Michael Moran

The doorbell jarred me
toward consciousness
on a sultry Sunday morning
when I was nineteen,
a college sophomore.
I had slept where the bourbon
laid me—on an old couch
reclaimed from a curb.
The party had sped by,
left me road-kill,
limp and snoring,
so my roommates said,
and now I stumbled
to the buzzing door,
remembering what I had never
completely forgotten—
my family is coming.

Dad at the door.
I mumble, "I overslept,"
as he surveys the wreckage
of these tired rooms:
lip-sticked cigarette butts,
crushed aluminum cans,
glasses floating sliced limes,
broken brown bottles,
a sticky wooden floor under

smoked-and-perfumed air.
He turns slowly to me
and winks! 'We can't
let your mother see this,'
as if we'd planned the party
together, drank from the same
Yellowstone bottle all night.

We spring to action,
sponging spills, opening windows,
gathering garbage. He spins
through the rooms
with the grace of a dancer—
a miniature Falstaff—
humming old barroom songs
from his Navy days,
chuckling softly, his eyes
gleaming as he hides
the half-emptied Jim Beam.
By the time my mother
has herded all my siblings
up the stairs to the apartment,
we have salvaged it to decency.

You see, he thought I was
too serious, worried that I
read too many books, never
got into real trouble.
I remember the way
he stared at me
one Halloween evening
when I told him
I was staying home
to read King Lear.

His cold brown eyes
were sad, disgusted,
the eyes of an Elizabethan
reveler who had just heard
that the Puritans
had closed the theatres.

But that morning
I made him proud,
couldn't have done better,
unless, perhaps,
one of the girls
had slept over
and answered the door,
wearing nothing
but my faded
red flannel shirt,
top buttons
undone.

Spring Rain

Kenneth Rexroth

The smoke of our campfire lowers
And coagulates under
The redwoods, like low-lying
Clouds. Fine mist fills the air. Drops
Rattle down from all the leaves.
As the evening comes on
The treetops vanish in fog.
Two saw-whet owls utter their
Metallic sobbing cries high
Overhead. As it gets dark
The mist turns to rain. We are
All alone in the forest.
No one is near us for miles.
In the firelight mice scurry
Hunting crumbs. Tree toads cry like
Tiny owls. Deer snort in the
Underbrush. Their eyes are green
In the firelight like balls of
Foxfire. This morning I read
Mei Yao Chen's poems, all afternoon
We walked along the stream through
Woods and meadows full of June
Flowers. We chased frogs in the
Pools and played with newts and young
Grass snakes. I picked a wild rose
For your hair. You brought

New flowers for me to name.
Now it is night and our fire
Is a red throat open in
The profound blackness, full of
The throb and hiss of the rain.

Sleeping Next to the Man on the Plane

Ellen Bass

I'm not well. Neither is he.
Periodically he pulls out a handkerchief
and blows his nose. I worry
about germs, but appreciate how he shares
the armrest—especially
considering his size—too large
to lay the tray over his lap.
His seatbelt barely buckles. At least
he doesn't have to ask for an extender
for which I imagine him grateful. Our upper arms
press against each other, like apricots growing
from the same node. My arm is warm
where his touches it. I close my eyes.
In the chilly, oxygen-poor air, I am glad
to be close to his breathing mass.
We want our own species. We want
to lie down next to our own kind.
Even here in this metal encumbrance, hurtling
improbably 30,000 feet above the earth,
with all this civilization—down
to the chicken-or-lasagna in their
environmentally-incorrect packets,
even as the woman behind me is swiping
her credit card on the phone embedded
in my headrest and the folks in first

are watching their individual movies
on personal screens, I lean
into this stranger, seeking primitive comfort—
heat, touch, breath—as we slip
into the ancient vulnerability of sleep.

Starfish

Eleanor Lerman

This is what life does. It lets you walk up to
the store to buy breakfast and the paper, on a
stiff knee. It lets you choose the way you have
your eggs, your coffee. Then it sits a fisherman
down beside you at the counter who says, Last night
the channel was full of starfish. And you wonder,
is this a message, finally, or just another day?

Life lets you take the dog for a walk down to the
pond, where whole generations of biological
processes are boiling beneath the mud. Reeds
speak to you of the natural world: they whisper,
they sing. And herons pass by. Are you old
enough to appreciate the moment? Too old?
There is movement beneath the water, but it
may be nothing. There may be nothing going on.

And then life suggests that you remember the
years you ran around, the years you developed
a shocking lifestyle, advocated careless abandon,
owned a chilly heart. Upon reflection, you are
genuinely surprised to find how quiet you have
become. And then life lets you go home to think
about all this. Which you do, for quite a long time.

Later, you wake up beside your old love, the one
who never had any conditions, the one who waited

you out. This is life's way of letting you know that
you are lucky. (It won't give you smart or brave,
so you'll have to settle for lucky.) Because you
were born at a good time. Because you
were able to listen when people spoke to you. Because you
stopped when you should have started again.

So life lets you have a sandwich, and pie for your
late night dessert. (Pie for the dog, as well.) And
then life sends you back to bed, to dreamland,
while outside, the starfish drift through the channel,
with smiles on their starry faces as they head
out to deep water, to the far and boundless sea.

Summer Night, Riverside

Sara Teasdale

In the wild soft summer darkness
How many and many a night we two together
Sat in the park and watched the Hudson
Wearing her lights like golden spangles
Glinting on black satin.
The rail along the curving pathway
Was low in a happy place to let us cross,
And down the hill a tree that dripped with bloom
Sheltered us,
While your kisses and the flowers,
Falling, falling,
Tangled in my hair . . .

The frail white stars moved slowly over the sky.

And now, far off
In the fragrant darkness
The tree is tremulous again with bloom
For June comes back.

To-night what girl
Dreamily before her mirror shakes from her hair
This year's blossoms, clinging to its coils?

The Wedding Vow

Sharon Olds

I did not stand at the altar, I stood
at the foot of the chancel steps, with my beloved,
and the minister stood on the top step
holding the open Bible. The church
was wood, painted ivory inside, no people—God's
stable perfectly cleaned. It was night,
spring—outside, a moat of mud,
and inside, from the rafters, flies
fell onto the open Bible, and the minister
tilted it and brushed them off. We stood
beside each other, crying slightly
with fear and awe. In truth, we had married
that first night, in bed, we had been
married by our bodies, but now we stood
in history—what our bodies had said,
mouth to mouth, we now said publicly,
gathered together, death. We stood
holding each other by the hand, yet I also
stood as if alone, for a moment,
just before the vow, though taken
years before, took. It was a vow
of the present and the future, and yet I felt it
to have some touch on the distant past
or the distant past on it, I felt
the wordless, dry, crying ghost of my
parents' marriage there, somewhere

in the echoing space—perhaps one of the
plummeting flies, bouncing slightly
as it hit *forsaking all others*, then was brushed
away. I felt as if I had come
to claim a promise—the sweetness I'd inferred
from their sourness, and at the same time that I
had come, congenitally unworthy, to beg.
And yet, I had been working toward this hour
all my life. And then it was time
to speak—he was offering me, no matter
what, his life. That is all I had to
do, that evening, to accept the gift
I had longed for—to say I had accepted it,
as if being asked if I breathe. Do I take?
I do. I take as he takes—we have been
practicing this. Do you bear this pleasure? I do.

John Green Takes His Warner, New Hampshire, Neighbor to a Red Sox Game

Maxine Kumin

Everett down the hill's
52 and trim. No beer gut.
Raises beef, corn, hay, cuts
cordwood between harvests.
Goes to bed at 8 and falls
into sleep like a parachutist.

He's never been to a ballgame.
He's never been to Boston though
he went over to Portland Maine
one time ten, fifteen years ago.

In Sullivan Square, they
luck out, find a space
for John's car, take
the T to Fenway Park.
The famous T!
A kind of underground trolley.
Runs in the dark.
No motorman that Ev can see.
Jammed with other sports fans.

John has to show him
how to put the token in.
How to press with his hips
to go through the turnstile.

How to stand back while
the doors whoosh shut.
How to grab a strap
as the car pitches forward.
How to push out
with the surging crowd.

Afterward Ev says the game's
a whole lot better on tv.
Too many fans.
Too many other folks for him.

Mount Kearsarge Shines

Donald Hall

Mount Kearsarge shines with ice; from hemlock branches
snow slides onto snow; no stream, creek, or river
           budges but remains still. Tonight
                  we carry armloads of logs

from woodshed to Glenwood and build up the fire
that keeps the coldest night outside our windows.
           Sit by the woodstove, Camilla,
                  while I bring glasses of white,

and we'll talk, passing the time, about weather
without pretending that we can alter it:
           Storms stop when they stop, no sooner,
                  leaving the birches glossy

with ice and bent glittering to rimy ground.
We'll avoid the programmed weatherman grinning
           from the box, cheerful with tempest,
                  and take the day as it comes.

one day at a time, the way everyone says.
These hours are the best because we hold them close
           in our uxorious nation.
                  Soon we'll walk—when days turn fair

and frost stays off—over old roads, listening
for peepers as spring comes on, never to miss
        the day's offering of pleasure
                        for the government of two.

Arc

Amy M. Clark

My seatmate on the late-night flight
could have been my father. I held
a biography, but he wanted to talk.
The pages closed around my finger
on my spot, and as we inclined
into the sky, we went backwards
in his life, beginning with five hours
before, the funeral for his only brother,
a forgotten necktie in his haste
to catch this plane the other way
just yesterday, his wife at home
caring for a yellow Lab she'd found
along the road by the olive grove,
and the pretty places we had visited—
Ireland for me, Germany for him—
a village where he served his draft
during the Korean War, and would like
to see again to show his wife
how lucky he had been. He talked
to me and so we held
his only brother's death at bay.
I turned off my reading light,
remembering another veteran
I met in a pine forest years ago
who helped me put my tent up
in the wind. What was I thinking

camping there alone? I was grateful
he kept watch across the way
and served coffee in a blue tin cup.
Like the makeshift shelter of a tent,
a plane is brought down,
but as we folded to the ground,
I had come to appreciate
even my seatmate's breath, large
and defenseless, the breath of a man
who hadn't had a good night's rest.
I listened and kept the poles
from blowing down, and kept
a vigil from the dark to day.

Why I Have A Crush On You, UPS Man

Alice N. Persons

you bring me all the things I order
are never in a bad mood
always have a jaunty wave as you drive away
look good in your brown shorts
we have an ideal uncomplicated relationship
you're like a cute boyfriend with great legs
who always brings the perfect present
(why, it's just what I've always wanted!)
and then is considerate enough to go away
oh, UPS Man, let's hop in your clean brown truck and elope!
ditch your job, I'll ditch mine
let's hit the road for Brownsville
and tempt each other
with all the luscious brown foods—
roast beef, dark chocolate,
brownies, Guinness, homemade pumpernickel, molasses cookies
I'll make you my mama's bourbon pecan pie
we'll give all the packages to kind looking strangers
live in a cozy wood cabin
with a brown dog or two
and a black and brown tabby
I'm serious, UPS Man. Let's do it.
Where do I sign?

My Love for All Things
Warm and Breathing

William Kloefkorn

I have seldom loved more than one thing at a time,
yet this morning I feel myself expanding, each
part of me soft and glandular, and under my skin
is room enough now for the loving of many things,
and all of them at once, these students especially,
not only the girl in the yellow sweater, whose
name, Laura Buxton, is somehow the girl herself,
Laura for the coy green mellowing eyes, Buxton
for all the rest, but also the simple girl in blue
on the back row, her mouth sad beyond all reasonable
inducements, and the boy with the weight problem,
his teeth at work even now on his lower lip, and
the grand profusion of hair and nails and hands and
legs and tongues and thighs and fingertips and
wrists and throats, yes, of throats especially,
throats through which passes the breath that joins
the air that enters through these ancient windows,
that exits, that takes with it my own breath, inside
this room just now my love for all things warm and
breathing, that lifts it high to scatter it fine and
enormous into the trees and the grass, into the heat
beneath the earth beneath the stone, into the
boundless lust of all things bound but gathering.

San Antonio

Naomi Shihab Nye

Tonight I lingered over your name,
the delicate assembly of vowels
a voice inside my head.
You were sleeping when I arrived.
I stood by your bed
and watched the sheets rise gently.
I knew what slant of light
would make you turn over.
It was then I felt
the highways slide out of my hands.
I remembered the old men
in the west side cafe,
dealing dominoes like magical charms.
It was then I knew,
like a woman looking backward,
I could not leave you,
or find anyone I loved more.

They Sit Together on the Porch

Wendell Berry

They sit together on the porch, the dark
Almost fallen, the house behind them dark.
Their supper done with, they have washed and dried
The dishes–only two plates now, two glasses,
Two knives, two forks, two spoons—small work for two.
She sits with her hands folded in her lap,
At rest. He smokes his pipe. They do not speak,
And when they speak at last it is to say
What each one knows the other knows. They have
One mind between them, now, that finally
For all its knowing will not exactly know
Which one goes first through the dark doorway, bidding
Goodnight, and which sits on a while alone.

As Toilsome I Wander'd Virginia's Woods

Walt Whitman

As toilsome I wander'd Virginia's woods,
To the music of rustling leaves, kick'd by my feet, (for 'twas
    autumn,)
I mark'd at the foot of a tree the grave of a soldier;
Mortally wounded he and buried on the retreat, (easily all could
    understand;)
The halt of a mid-day hour, when up! no time to lose
    —yet this sign left,
On a tablet scrawl'd and nail'd on the tree by the grave,
Bold, cautious, true, and my loving comrade.

Long, long I muse, then on my way go wandering;
Many a changeful season to follow, and many a scene of life;
Yet at times through changeful season and scene, abrupt,
    alone, or in the crowded street,
Comes before me the unknown soldier's grave—comes the
    inscription rude in Virginia's woods,
Bold, cautious, true, and my loving comrade.

Only Years

Kenneth Rexroth

I come back to the cottage in
Santa Monica Canyon where
Andrée and I were poor and
Happy together. Sometimes we
Were hungry and stole vegetables
From the neighbors' gardens.
Sometimes we went out and gathered
Cigarette butts by flashlight.
But we went swimming every day,
All year round. We had a dog
Called Proclus, a vast yellow
Mongrel, and a white cat named
Cyprian. We had our first
Joint art show, and they began
To publish my poems in Paris.
We worked under the low umbrella
Of the acacia in the dooryard.
Now I get out of the car
And stand before the house in the dusk.
The acacia blossoms powder the walk
With little pills of gold wool.
The odor is drowsy and thick
In the early evening.
The tree has grown twice as high
As the roof. Inside, an old man
And woman sit in the lamplight.

I go back and drive away
To Malibu Beach and sit
With a grey-haired childhood friend and
Watch the full moon rise over the
Long rollers wrinkling the dark bay.

6

A COMFORTING
IMMENSITY

The Light by the Barn

William Stafford

The light by the barn that shines all night
pales at dawn when a little breeze comes.

A little breeze comes breathing the fields
from their sleep and waking the slow windmill.

The slow windmill sings the long day
about anguish and loss to the chickens at work.

The little breeze follows the slow windmill
and the chickens at work till the sun goes down—

Then the light by the barn again.

One Home

William Stafford

Mine was a Midwest home—you can keep your world.
Plain black hats rode the thoughts that made our code.
We sang hymns in the house; the roof was near God.

The light bulb that hung in the pantry made a wan light,
but we could read by it the names of preserves—
outside, the buffalo grass, and the wind in the night.

A wildcat sprang at Grandpa on the Fourth of July
when he was cutting plum bushes for fuel,
before Indians pulled the West over the edge of the sky.

To anyone who looked at us we said, "My friend";
liking the cut of a thought, we could say "Hello."
(But plain black hats rode the thoughts that made our code.)

The sun was over our town; it was like a blade.
Kicking cottonwood leaves we ran toward storms.
Wherever we looked the land would hold us up.

To make a prairie

Emily Dickinson

To make a prairie it takes a clover and one bee,
One clover, and a bee.
And revery.
The revery alone will do,
If bees are few.

Silence in North Dakota

Bill Holm

On the lip of the Killdeer Canyon
five hundred feet over the tan buttes
that flank the little Missouri
in the middle of North Dakota
in the middle of North America
in the middle of the western hemisphere
on tax day in the middle of April
at almost the end of the second millennium
the universe held its breath
for a full minute.

Complete, inviolate silence—
not a crow cawed
not a frog croaked
the wind shut its mouth
the cars and tractors stopped
the TVs all went dead
words failed for no good reason
clouds scudded but kept quiet about it
and everything alive or
what is sometimes called not-alive
listened to everything else
stones, motors, crocuses, blood pulsing
And then the crow cawed,

(that seemed to be the signal)
and the universe exhaled
and everything started again
but for that minute we heard
what it was really like.

At the Un-National Monument Along the Canadian Border

William Stafford

This is the field where the battle did not happen,
where the unknown soldier did not die.
This is the field where grass joined hands,
where no monument stands,
and the only heroic thing is the sky.

Birds fly here without any sound,
unfolding their wings across the open.
No people killed—or were killed—on this ground
hallowed by neglect and an air so tame
that people celebrate it by forgetting its name.

Farmhouses, Iowa

Baron Wormser

Invariably, a family in each one
And someone opening the fridge to fetch
A carton of milk, someone sitting in
A chair and shelling peas, someone looking

Out a window at a barn, two willow trees.
Solitude broods like a pursuing shadow;
A radio fades in and out—the voice
Eager yet eerie. Three ages anchor

The oaken dinner table: Mom and Dad
Up-before-dawn weary, Grandma perturbed
About half-thawed rolls, the children recounting
School stories, then silent. In the parlor
A whiskey tumbler rests beside a Bible.
The old collie whimpers when a car goes by.

Dishwater

Ted Kooser

Slap of the screen door, flat knock
of my grandmother's boxy black shoes
on the wooden stoop, the hush and sweep
of her knob-kneed, cotton-aproned stride
out to the edge and then, toed in
with a furious twist and heave,
a bridge that leaps from her hot red hands
and hangs there shining for fifty years
over the mystified chickens,
over the swaying nettles, the ragweed,
the clay slope down to the creek,
over the redwing blackbirds in the tops
of the willows, a glorious rainbow
with an empty dishpan swinging at one end.

Some Directions for the December Touring of Westcentral Nebraska

William Kloefkorn

Turn right at the Standard Station
And head due west. Do not
Eat at the Hungry Indian
In Ogallala or stop for

Free tea at the Big Farmer
In Oshkosh—By Gosh. My
Advice, Sir: go cold and
Hungry over these wintered ranges

Where only on a cloudless night
Can the sky outstrip the land.
Join the tumbleweed. Huddle
With herefords against leeward

Walls. Walk barefoot over
Steaming dung along the
Dormant seeded rows of
Next year's yield. Forget

The motels at North Platte,
Tune out all noisy Teepees:
KODY, KOLT, KCOW. Hum
The notes of rusting cultivators

And watch with the hawk
for mice and rabbits and
Scott's once-in-a-lifetime bluff.
Inhale. Go dizzy with the

Windmill. Stretch even the
Fingertips against sand-coated hills.
You can get there from here,
Sir. But you must go

Cold and hungry. That route is best
Just forget your Pontiac, then
Turn right at the Standard Station
and drive due west.

Tornado Weather

Vincent Wixon

1.

Clouds build all day,
hold west of the section.
Plowing east he feels them
piling darker, deeper.

Wind through ankle high corn
comes cold, dries his back,
and he pushes the throttle a notch,
checks the hills blurring between the wheels.

At the field's end he raises the shovels,
as first drops darken his shirt.
He shifts into high and opens the engine for home.
The rain thickens, turns hard,
pings off the tractor, bounces on the road,
stings his bent head and back.

He pulls under the cottonwood,
covers the stack with a can,
and sprints for the barn.

2.

Clouds hang low and come on—
a black-green curtain wide as sky.
The high leaves of the cottonwoods
shudder for the first time all day.

Women stand on their porches
and the air turns cool.
They shiver, hug their sleeveless arms,

and listen for the tractor-whine
of their husbands leaving the fields.
They call the children from the barn,
and turn inside to switch on the radio.

A Wife Explains Why She Likes Country

Barbara Ras

Because those cows in the bottomland are black and white, colors
anyone can understand, even against the green
of the grass, where they glide like yes and no,
    nothing in between,
because in country, heartache has nowhere to hide,
it's the Church of Abundant Life, the Alamo,
the hubbub of the hoi polloi, the parallel lines of rail fences,
because I like rodeos more than I like golf,
because there's something about the sound of mealworms and
leeches and the dream of a double-wide
that reminds me this is America, because of the simple pleasure
of a last chance, because sometimes whiskey
tastes better than wine, because hauling hogs on the road
is as good as it gets when the big bodies are layered
    like pigs in a cake,
not one layer but two,
because only country has a gun with a full choke
    and a slide guitar
that melts playing it cool into sweaty surrender in one note,
because in country you can smoke forever and it'll never kill you,
because roadbeds, flatbeds, your bed or mine,
because the package store is right across from the chicken plant
and it sells boiled peanuts, because I'm fixin' to wear boots
    to the dance
and make my hair bigger, because no smarty-pants,
    just easy rhymes,

perfect love, because I'm lost deep within myself and the sad songs
    call me out,
because even you with your superior aesthetic cried
when Tammy Wynette died,
because my people
come from dirt.

A Small Excursion

Mona Van Duyn

Take a trip with me
through the towns in Missouri.
Feel naming in all its joy
as we go through Braggadocio, Barks, Kidder, Fair Play,
Bourbon, Bean Lake
and Loose Creek.
If we should get lost
we could spend the night at
Lutesville, Brinktown, Excello, Nodaway,
Humansville or Kinderpost.

If we liked Bachelor we could bypass
with only slight compunction
another interesting place,
Conception Junction.

I think you would feel instant intimacy
with all the little flaws
of an Elmer, Esther, Ethel, Oscar or Archie,
all the quirky ways
of a Eunice or a Bernice,
at home in a
Hattie or even an Amazonia.

I'd enjoy, wouldn't you, saying that I came from
Chloride, or Map or Boss or Turtle
Or Arab or Chamois or Huzzah or Drum.

Surely the whole world loves the lover of men
who calls a tiny gathering
in midwest America
Paris, Carthage or Alexandria,
Odessa, Cairo, Arcadia or Milan,
as well as the one who calls
his clump of folk
Postoak,
the literalist who aims low
and calls it Shortbend or Old Mines
or Windyville or Iron or Nobby or Gumbo.

Riding along together,
we could think of all we'd had
at both Blooming Rose and Evening Shade.
Heading into the setting sun,
the gravel roads might get long and rough,
but we could make the difficult choice between
Minimum and Enough,
between Protem and Longrun.
And if it got very late
we could stay at Stet.

Isn't there something infinitely appealing
in the candor
of calling a collection of human beings
Liberal, Clever, Bland, or
Moody, Useful, Handy, or
Rich, Fertile and Fair dealing?
People who named these towns
were nobody's fools.
Passing through Peculiar, we could follow
a real school bus labelled Peculiar Public Schools.

O to be physically and aesthetically
footloose,
travelling always,
going through
pure sound that stands for a space,
like Cabool, Canalou, Plad, Auxvasse,
Koshkonong, Weaubleau, Roubidoux,
Hahn Dongola, Knob Noster and Foose!

Midwest

Stephen Dunn

After the paintings of David Ahlsted

We have lived in this town,
have disappeared
on this prairie. The church

always was smaller
than the grain elevator,
though we pretended otherwise.
The houses were similar

because few of us wanted
to be different
or estranged. And the sky

would never forgive us,
no matter how many times
we guessed upwards
in the dark.

The sky was the prairie's
double, immense,
kaleidoscopic, cold.

The town was where
and how we huddled
against such forces,
and the old abandoned

pickup on the edge
of town was how we knew
we had gone too far,
or had returned.

People? Now we can see them,
invisible in their houses
or in their stores.

Except for one man
lounging on his porch,
they are part of the buildings,

they have determined
every stubborn shape, the size
of each room. The trailer home
with the broken window

is somebody's life.
One thing always is
more important than another,

this empty street, this vanishing
point. The good eye knows
no democracy. Shadows follow

sunlight as they should,
as none of us can prevent.
Everything is conspicuous
and is not.

In Texas

May Sarton

In Texas the lid blew off the sky a long time ago
So there's nothing to keep the wind from blowing
And it blows all the time. Everywhere is far to go
So there's no hurry at all, and no reason for going.
In Texas there's so much space words have a way
Of getting lost in the silence before they're spoken
So people hang on a long time to what they have to say;
And when they say it the silence is not broken,
But it absorbs the words and slowly gives them
Over to miles of white-gold plains and gray-green hills,
And they are part of that silence that outlives them.
Nothing moves fast in Texas except the windmills
And the hawk that rises up with a clatter of wings.
(Nothing more startling here than sudden motion,
Everything is so still.) But the earth slowly swings
In time like a great swelling never-ending ocean,
And the houses that ride the tawny waves get smaller
As you get near them because you see them then
Under the whole sky, and the whole sky is so much taller
With the lid off than a million towers built by men.
After a while you can only see what's at horizon's edge,
And you are stretched with looking so far instead of near,
So you jump, you are startled by a blown piece of sedge;
You feel wide-eyed and ruminative as a ponderous steer.
In Texas you look at America with a patient eye.
You want everything to be sure and slow and set in relation
To immense skies and earth that never ends. You wonder why

People must talk and strain so much about a nation
That lives in spaces vaster than a man's dream and can go
Five hundred miles through wilderness, meeting only the hawk
And the dead rabbit in the road. What happens must be slow,
Must go deeper even than hand's work or tongue's talk,
Must rise out of the flesh like sweat after a hard day,
Must come slowly, in its own time, in its own way.

Squatting

Robert Morgan

The men in rural places when
they stop to talk and visit will
not stand, for that would make it seem
they're in a rush. Nor will they sit
on ground that might be cold or wet.
Instead they squat with dignity
on heels close to the ground and chat
for hours. And while they tell and answer,
or listen, hunkered out of wind,
they draw with sticks in dirt a map
to illustrate a story or
show evidence for argument.
They sketch out patterns, write on dirt
and doodle vague arithmetic,
who never will take up a pen
on page or slate or canvas. They
will absentmindedly make shapes
and figures of their reveries
and rub them out again complete
to give their art no status of
attention in the casual toss
of discourse, open forum of
community, out there on bare
familiar ground where generations
have squatted, called it ownership.

Farley, Iowa

from "Standing by Stones"

Christopher Wiseman

The farm is gone. The Comer farm is gone.
Your mother's brother, Uncle Joe, has sold it.
He's old now and his kids don't want to farm,
Have different lives in towns. He has coins, too,
From Somerset. His grandfather's. We sit for the last
Time in the farm kitchen, driven for days
To get here before he finally moves out,
Summer lightning starting, the way it does,
The evening air heavy, full of growth.
Joe will move. There's sadness in us all.
And you, my wife, drinking all of this in,
Talking about our children, asking Joe
About the Iowa you left, the people,
The whole big thing that was your life, your childhood.
You used to bike here, on the gravel roads,
From Cascade, for lemonade and ice cream, to see
The barns, the animals. Back in the fifties.
He got to here from Somerset, that man.
Joe talks about the richness of the soil,
Blizzards, tornadoes, heat beyond belief,
Guesses about ships and wagons, breaking the land,
Clearing stones from grass. His grandfather.
What will you do without the farm, you ask him.
I'll be fine, he says. Live somewhere else.

From Here to There

Brad Leithauser

There are those great winds on a tear
Over the Great Plains,
Bending the grasses all the way
Down to the roots
And the grasses revealing
A gracefulness in the wind's fury
You would not otherwise
Have suspected there.

And there's the wind off the sea
Roiling the thin crowns of the great
Douglas firs on the cragged
Oregon coast, uprooting
Choruses of outraged cries,
As if the trees were unused
To bending, that can weather
Such storms for a century.

And—somewhere between those places,
Needing a break—we climb out stiff
From our endless drive to stand, dwindled,
On a ridge, holding hands,
In what are foothills only because
The neighboring mountains are
So much taller, and there are the breezes,
Contrarily pulled, awakening our faces.

Crossing Kansas by Train

Donald Justice

The telephone poles
Have been holding their
Arms out
A long time now
To birds
That will not
Settle there
But pass with
Strange cawings
Westward to
Where dark trees
Gather about a
Water hole this
Is Kansas the
Mountains start here
Just behind
The closed eyes
Of a farmer's
Sons asleep
In their work clothes

Crossing Central Illinois

Alvin Greenberg

Life after all is fair; ultimately it breaks everybody's heart.
—Rachel Maddux

here's this land so flat the rain it can't soak up
just puddles where it falls on either side of the interstate

life goes on with no horizon except the vague grey wall
the fog constructs today, behind which people even older than

myself might be sitting down to lunch now. i wonder why.
can there be sustenance here? between plowed-under cornfields

and the lay-offs at the caterpillar factory? it's all so
thin, as if the winter sky's come down and pressed

this land so flat the rain it can't soak up just puddles
where it falls. a film of water on a film of earth.

you can't slip the skin off a boiled new potato
any slicker than how it all slides away here. believe me,

there's nothing we can do to keep anything from happening:
the earth compresses and releases at its own rate:

no sense calling that breathing. i knew someone
who really did see angels once; they danced across a field

of purple clover and kept her going for twenty years or so
until the gin waltzed in. now it's work, work, work.

look at this thin strip of light we slide along at sixty
. . . sixty something: years or miles per hour, what

truth or sense there is spread out on either side like fog
along a land so flat the rain it can't soak up just

puddles where it falls. we look at it. it looks back at us.
this is how we know ourselves. that is how we know the world.

Island Cities

John Updike

You see them from airplanes, nameless green islands
in the oceanic, rectilinear plains,
twenty or thirty blocks, compact, but with
everything needed visibly in place—
the high-school playing fields, the swatch of park
along the crooked river, the feeder highways,
the main drag like a zipper, outlying malls
sliced from dirt-colored cakes of plowed farmland.

Small lives, we think—pat, flat—in such tight grids.
But, much like brains with every crease CAT-scanned,
these cities keep their secrets: vagaries
of the spirit, groundwater that floods
the nearby quarries and turns them skyey blue,
dewdrops of longing, jewels boxed in these blocks.

Home Town

William Stafford

Peace on my little town, a speck in the safe,
    comforting, impersonal immensity of Kansas.
Benevolence like a gentle haze on its courthouse
    (the model of Greek pillars to me)
    on its quiet little bombshell of a library,
    on its continuous, hidden, efficient sewer system.

Sharp, amazed, steadfast regard on its more upright citizenry,
    my nosy, incredible, delicious neighbors.

Haunting invasion of a train whistle to my friends,
    moon-gilding, regular breaths of the old memories to
        them—
    the old whispers, old attempts, old beauties, ever new.

Peace on my little town, haze-blessed, sun-friended,
    dreaming sleepy days under the world-champion sky.

Lawrence, Kansas
c. Fall 1941

Highway Hypothesis

Maxine Kumin

Nothing quite rests the roving eye
like this long view of sloping fields
that rise to a toyshop farmhouse
with matchstick barns and sheds.
A large yellow beetle spits silage
onto an upturned cricket while
several inch-high cars and trucks
flow soundlessly up the spitcurl drive.

Bucophilia, I call it—
nostalgia over a pastoral vista—
where for all I know the farmer
who owns it or rents it just told his
wife he'd kill her if she left him and
she did and he did and now here come
the auctioneer, the serious bidders
and an ant-train of gawking onlookers.

Flying at Night

Ted Kooser

Above us, stars. Beneath us, constellations.
Five billion miles away, a galaxy dies
like a snowflake falling on water. Below us,
some farmer, feeling the chill of that distant death,
snaps on his yard light, drawing his sheds and barn
back into the little system of his care.
All night, the cities, like shimmering novas,
tug with bright streets at lonely lights like his.

7

A SORT OF RAPTURE

Above Pate Valley

Gary Snyder

We finished clearing the last
Section of trail by noon,
High on the ridge-side
Two thousand feet above the creek
Reached the pass, went on
Beyond the white pine groves,
Granite shoulders, to a small
Green meadow watered by the snow,
Edged with Aspen—sun
Straight high and blazing
But the air was cool.
Ate a cold fried trout in the
Trembling shadows. I spied
A glitter, and found a flake
Black volcanic glass—obsidian—
By a flower. Hands and knees
Pushing the Bear grass, thousands
Of arrowhead leavings over a
Hundred yards. Not one good
Head, just razor flakes
On a hill snowed all but summer,
A land of fat summer deer,
They came to camp. On their
Own trails. I followed my own
Trail here. Picked up the cold-drill,
Pick, singlejack, and sack
Of dynamite.
Ten thousand years.

V

Wendell Berry

For Maxine Kumin

Raking hay on a rough slope,
when I was about sixteen,
I drove to the ridgetop and saw
in a neighbor's field on the other side
a pond in a swale, and around it
the whole field filled
with chicory in bloom, blue
as the sky reflected in the pond—
bluer even, and somehow lighter,
though they belonged to gravity.
They were the morning's
blossoms and would not last.
But I go back now in my mind
to when I drew the long windrow
to the top of the rise, and I see
the blue-flowered field, holding
in its center the sky-reflecting pond.
It seems, as then, another world
in this world, such as a pilgrim
might travel days and years
to find, and find at last
on the morning of his return
by his mere being at home
awake—a moment seen, forever known.

The Word

Maxine Kumin

We ride up softly to the hidden
oval in the woods, a plateau rimmed
with wavy stands of gray birch and white pine,
my horse thinking his thoughts, happy
in the October dapple, and I thinking
mine-and-his, which is my prerogative,

both of us just in time to see a big doe
loft up over the four-foot fence, her white scut
catching the sun and then releasing it,
soundlessly clapping our reveries shut.
The pine grove shivers as she passes.
The red squirrels thrill, announcing her departure.

Come back! I want to call to her,
we who mean you no harm. Come back and show us
who stand pinned in stopped time to the track
how you can go from a standing start
up and over. We on our side, pulses racing
are synchronized with your racing heart.

I want to tell her, Watch me
mornings when I fill the cylinders
with sunflower seeds, see how the chickadees
and lesser redbreasted nuthatches crowd
onto my arm, permitting me briefly
to stand in for a tree,

and how the vixen in the bottom meadow
I ride across allows me under cover
of horse scent to observe the education
of her kits, how they dive for the burrow
on command, how they re-emerge at another
word she uses, a word I am searching for.

Its sound is o-shaped and unencumbered,
the see-through color of river,
airy as the topmost evergreen fingers
and soft as pine duff underfoot
where the doe lies down out of sight;
take me in, tell me the word.

The Evening Is Tranquil,
and Dawn Is a Thousand Miles Away

Charles Wright

The mares go down for their evening feed
>   into the meadow grass.
Two pine trees sway the invisible wind—
>   some sway, some don't sway.
The heart of the world lies open, leached and ticking with sunlight
For just a minute or so.
The mares have their heads on the ground,
>   the trees have their heads on the blue sky.
Two ravens circle and twist.
>   On the borders of heaven, the river flows clear a bit longer.

Riding Out at Evening

Linda McCarriston

At dusk, everything blurs and softens.
From here out over the long valley,
the fields and hills pull up
the first slight sheets of evening,
as, over the next hour,
heavier, darker ones will follow.

Quieted roads, predictable deer
browsing in a neighbor's field, another's
herd of heifers, the kitchen lights
starting in many windows. On horseback
I take it in, neither visitor
nor intruder, but kin passing, closer
and closer to night, its cold streams
rising in the sugarbush and hollow.

Half-aloud, I say to the horse,
or myself, or whoever: let fire not come
to this house, nor that barn,
nor lightning strike the cattle.
Let dogs not gain the gravid doe, let the lights
of the rooms convey what they seem to.

And who is to say it is useless
or foolish to ride out in the falling light

alone, wishing, or praying,
for particular good to particular beings,
on one small road in a huge world?
The horse bears me along, like grace,

making me better than what I am,
and what I think or say or see
is whole in these moments, is neither
small nor broken. For up, out of
the inscrutable earth, have come my body
and the separate body of the mare:
flawed and aching and wronged. Who then
is better made to say *be well, be glad,*

or who to long that we, as one,
might course over the entire valley,
over all valleys, as a bird in a great embrace
of flight, who presses against her breast,
in grief and tenderness,
the whole weeping body of the world?

Winter: Tonight: Sunset

David Budbill

Tonight at sunset walking on the snowy road,
my shoes crunching on the frozen gravel, first

through the woods, then out into the open fields
past a couple of trailers and some pickup trucks, I stop

and look at the sky. Suddenly: orange, red, pink, blue,
green, purple, yellow, gray, all at once and everywhere.

I pause in this moment at the beginning of my old age
and I say a prayer of gratitude for getting to this evening

a prayer for being here, today, now, alive
in this life, in this evening, under this sky.

In the Bus

Grace Paley

Somewhere between Greenfield and Holyoke
snow became rain
and a child passed through me
as a person moves through mist
as the moon moves through
a dense cloud at night
as though I were cloud or mist
a child passed through me

On the highway that lies
across miles of stubble
and tobacco barns our bus speeding
speeding disordered the slanty rain
and a girl with no name   naked
wearing the last nakedness of
childhood   breathed in me
                    once   no
                    two breaths
a sigh   she whispered   Hey you
begin again
                    Again?
again   again   you'll see
it's easy   begin again   long ago

The Critic

C.K. Williams

In the Boston Public Library on Boylston Street, where all the
      bums come in stinking from the cold,
there was one who had a battered loose-leaf book he used to
      scribble in for hours on end.
He wrote with no apparent hesitation, quickly, and with
      concentration; his inspiration was inspiring:
you had to look again to realize that he was writing over words that
      were already there—
blocks of cursive etched into the softened paper, interspersed with
      poems in print he'd pasted in.
I hated to think of the volumes he'd violated to construct his opus,
      but I liked him anyway,
especially the way he'd often reach the end, close his work with
      weary satisfaction, then open again
and start again: page one, chapter one, his blood-rimmed eyes as
      rapt as David's doing psalms.

Late Spring

Jim Harrison

Because of the late, cold wet spring the fruit of greenness is sud-
denly upon us so that in Montana you can throw yourself down
just about anywhere on a green grassy bed, snooze on the riverbank
and wake to a yellow-rumped warbler flittering close to your head
then sipping a little standing water from a moose track. Of course
pitching yourself downward you first look for hidden rocks. Noth-
ing in nature is exactly suited to us. Meanwhile everywhere cows are
napping from overeating, and their frolicsome calves don't remem-
ber anything except this bounty. And tonight the calves will stare
at the full moon glistening off the mountain snow, both snow and
moon white as their mother's milk. This year the moisture has made
the peonies outside my studio so heavy with their beauty that they
droop to the ground and I think of my early love, Emily Brontë. The
cruelty of our different ages kept us apart. I tie and prop up the peo-
nies to prolong their lives, just as I would have nursed Emily so she
could see another spring.

Things I Know, Things I Don't

David Huddle

Virginia in early October
is a soft countryside, color not yet
in the trees but the leaves' green going pale,
the sunlight's angle sharp, the birds about
to move. Those cool mornings you catch a whiff
of woodsmoke, evenings you feel a chill
ring the air like a high, soft-blown flute note.
That season of my father's death was not
wrong, not wrong at all. If he had been well
that day he might have taken a walk with
Mother, one of their short strolls. Early that
morning there'd been heavy fog that was all
gone by nine. He'd have liked how that sun felt
on his shoulders. He'd have liked that weather.

The VCCA Fellows Visit the Holiness Baptist Church, Amherst, Virginia

Barbara Crooker

We are the only light faces in a sea of mahogany,
tobacco, almond, and this is not the only way
we are different. We've come in late, the choir
already singing, swaying to the music, moving
in the spirit. *When I was down, Lord, when
I was down, Jesus lifted me.* And, for a few minutes,
we are raised up, out of our own skepticism
and doubts, rising on the swell of their voices.
The singers sit, and we pass the peace, wrapped
in thick arms, ample bosoms, and I start to think
maybe God is a woman of color, and that She loves
us, in spite of our pale selves, so far away
from who we should really be. Parishioners
give testimonials, a deacon speaks of his sister,
who's "gone home," and I realize he doesn't mean
back to Georgia, but that she's passed over. I float
on this sweet certainty, of a return not to the bland
confection of wispy clouds and angels in nightshirts,
but to childhood's kitchen, a dew-drenched June
morning, roses tumbling by the back porch.
The preacher mounts the lectern, tells us he's been
up since four working at his other job, the one
that pays the bills, and he delivers a sermon
that lightens the heart, unencumbered by dogma
and theology. For the benediction, we all join hands,

visitors and strangers enfolded in the whole,
like raisins in sweet batter. We step through the door
into the stunning sunshine, and our hearts
lift out of our chests, tiny birds flying off to light
in the redbuds, to sing and sing and sing.

Resort, part IX

Patricia Hampl

The deluxe loneliness of September is here, slinking
    furs of fog, an ensemble punctuated by sapphires,
those few days more rash than the meridian of July,
    color-fast and glassy with light.
A whole month supported by the inherited gold of summer,
    the glamorous bright season.

The air is mushrooms and old heat, a stew of leaves
    and the shelled blossom-ends of raspberries.
Blueberries, by the railroad track, are black, reserved
    as shoes under the leggy foliage.
Some leaves are construction paper, some
    plastic gels dropped on the ground.

The rose was summer, the girlish flutter of pink,
    brazen pollen underneath it all, or I'd thought
it was the dead tongue of my first love, something
    romantic and vague slipping into sad green, past blossom.
But it is September, first frost, and the rose
    is a vegetable, practical as a widow, the stuff
of tea and a jam you buy in a health food store.
    Rose hips are more rose than the rose, more pink,
the jolly late apples of all that lyricism.
    The frank body of the flower unfolds its heart
which is pelvic, most beautiful bone,
    perfect gesture.

Never pick rose hips until after first frost:
    this rule you have observed. Now, the grass outside
the shack is crusted with the first lichen of frost.
    Now go ahead, harvest the rosy buttons, all
their lives packed into the shiny pouches. Inside,
    their pulp is orange as the season, the fire
that resides in every ripe, ready thing. Inside
    is the food, something useful.
What you were waiting for, what you kept touching,
    what you meant to say, meant to confide,
what your mother bears as her Celtic grudge,
    what the summer released, what each letter in the box
had as its further address, what the rose reveals,
    not rose, but rapture.

The Game

Marie Howe

And on certain nights,
maybe once or twice a year,
I'd carry the baby down
and all the kids would come
all nine of us together,
and we'd build a town in the basement

from boxes and blankets and overturned chairs.
And some lived under the pool table
or in the bathroom or the boiler room
or in the toy cupboard under the stairs,
and you could be a man or a woman
a husband or a wife or a child, and we bustled around
like a day in the village until

one of us turned off the lights, switch
by switch, and slowly it became night
and the people slept.

Our parents were upstairs with company or
not fighting, and one of us—it was usually
a boy—became the Town Crier,
and he walked around our little sleeping
population and tolled the hours with his voice,
and this was the game.

Nine o'clock and all is well, he'd say,
walking like a constable we must have seen
in a movie. And what we called an hour passed.
Ten o'clock and all is well.
And maybe somebody stirred in her sleep
or a grown up baby cried and was comforted . . .
Eleven o'clock and all is well.
Twelve o'clock. One o'clock. Two o'clock . . .

and it went on like that through the night we made up
until we could pretend it was morning.

Burning the Ditches

Jim Harrison

Over between Dillon and Butte in the valley near Melrose they're burning out the ditches on a moist, sad morning when my simple-minded heart aches for another life. Why can't I make a living trout fishing? The same question I posed sixty years ago to my father. I got drunk last night, an act now limited to about twice a year. It was the olive-skinned barmaid Nicole who set me off as if the dead filaments of my hormones had begun to twitch and wiggle again. In the morning I walk a canyon two-track and hear a canyon wren for the first time outside Arizona. Up the mountainside I see the long slender lines of the billowing smoke from the ditch fires, confused because the wren song is drawing me south to my winter life on the Mexican border. The ditches get choked with vegetation and they burn them in the spring so the irrigation water can flow freely. I suddenly determine that the smell of spring is the smell of the rushing river plus the billions of buds on trees and bushes. Back in the home ground, the Upper Peninsula of Michigan, when loggers went to town one day a month, they called getting drunk "burning out the grease." In 1958 a friend in San Francisco burned out his veins shooting up hot paregoric, a cheap high. It's safer for me to continue smoldering just below the temperature of actual flame wondering if there's a distant land where life freely flows like a river. Years ago in a high green pasture near timberline I watched a small black bear on its back rolling back and forth and shimmying to scratch its back, pawing the air with pleasure, not likely wanting to be anywhere or anyone else.

For All

Gary Snyder

Ah to be alive
    on a mid-September morn
    fording a stream
    barefoot, pants rolled up,
    holding boots, pack on,
    sunshine, ice in the shallows,
    northern rockies.

Rustle and shimmer of icy creek waters
stones turn underfoot, small and hard as toes
    cold nose dripping
    singing inside
    creek music, heart music,
    smell of sun on gravel.

    I pledge allegiance

I pledge allegiance to the soil
    of Turtle Island,
and to the beings who thereon dwell
    one ecosystem
    in diversity
    under the sun
With joyful interpenetration for all.

Thoreau and the Toads

David Wagoner

After the spring thaw, their voices ringing
    At dusk would beckon him through the meadow
        To the edge of their pond where, barefoot,
He would wade slowly into the water
    And stand there in the last of light
        To see the mating toads—a hundred or more
In the shallows around him, ignoring him
    Or taking him for another, inflating
        The pale-green bubbles of their throats to call
For *buffo terrestris*, leaping half out of the pool
    And scrambling to find partners. The atmosphere
        Would quiver with their harmonic over-
And undertones, with their loud, decent proposals
    Like the sounds of a church potluck, their invocations
        And offertories for disorderly conduct,
With the publishing of their indelicate banns
    And blessings to the needy in their distress
        And benedictions even beyond springtime
To all those of the faith. And he would see
    Among this communal rapture, there underwater,
        The small gray males lying silent
On the backs of females, holding on
    To their counterparts with every slippery finger
        And toe, both motionless, both gazing
Inward at the Indivisible
    And rising from time to time together
        To the surface only an inch above them

To breathe, then settling again and staring
    With such a consciousness of being
        Common American toads, he would stand beside them,
As content as they were with their medium
    Of exchange, the soles of his feet trembling
        With a resonance he could feel deep in his spine,
Believing this mud could be his altar too,
    And his pulpit, where all of his intentions
        Would be as clear as theirs, as clear as the air
In the chill of the fading light. He would lift
    His bare feet gently and silently, making scarcely
        A ripple, balancing
Himself onto the grass and, while his brethren
    Like a drunken choir went on
        And on without him, would sit down
Vibrant on the earth and once again struggle
    Into his stockings, into his waterproof boots,
        And straighten and square-knot his rawhide laces.

The Bridge

Henry Wadsworth Longfellow

I stood on the bridge at midnight,
    As the clocks were striking the hour,
And the moon rose o'er the city,
    Behind the dark church-tower.

I saw her bright reflection
    In the waters under me,
Like a golden goblet falling
    And sinking into the sea.

And far in the hazy distance
    Of that lovely night in June,
The blaze of the flaming furnace
    Gleamed redder than the moon.

Among the long, black rafters
    The wavering shadows lay,
And the current that came from the ocean
    Seemed to lift and bear them away;

As, sweeping and eddying through them,
    Rose the belated tide,
And, streaming into the moonlight,
    The seaweed floated wide.

And like those waters rushing
    Among the wooden piers,
A flood of thoughts came o'er me
    That filled my eyes with tears.

How often, O, how often,
    In the days that had gone by,
I had stood on that bridge at midnight
    And gazed on that wave and sky!

How often, O, how often,
    I had wished that the ebbing tide
Would bear me away on its bosom
    O'er the ocean wild and wide!

For my heart was hot and restless,
    And my life was full of care,
And the burden laid upon me
    Seemed greater than I could bear.

But now it has fallen from me,
    It is buried in the sea;
And only the sorrow of others
    Throws its shadow over me.

Yet whenever I cross the river
    On its bridge with wooden piers,
Like the odor of brine from the ocean
    Comes the thought of other years.

And I think how many thousands
    Of care-encumbered men,
Each bearing his burden of sorrow,
    Have crossed the bridge since then.

I see the long procession
    Still passing to and fro,
The young heart hot and restless,
    And the old subdued and slow!

And forever and forever,
    As long as the river flows,
As long as the heart has passions,
    As long as life has woes;

The moon and its broken reflection
    And its shadows shall appear,
As the symbol of love in heaven,
    And its wavering image here.

Autumn Waiting

Tom Hennen

Cold wind.
The day is waiting for winter
Without a sound.
Everything is waiting—
Broken-down cars in the dead weeds.
The weeds themselves.
Trees.
Even sunlight
Is in no hurry and stays
For a long time
On each cornstalk.
Blackbirds are silent
And sit in piles.
From a distance
They look like
Something
Spilled on the road.

This Morning

Raymond Carver

This morning was something. A little snow
lay on the ground. The sun floated in a clear
blue sky. The sea was blue, and blue-green,
as far as the eye could see.
Scarcely a ripple. Calm. I dressed and went
for a walk—determined not to return
until I took in what Nature had to offer.
I passed close to some old, bent-over trees.
Crossed a field strewn with rocks
where snow had drifted. Kept going
until I reached the bluff.
Where I gazed at the sea, and the sky, and
the gulls wheeling over the white beach
far below. All lovely. All bathed in a pure
cold light. But, as usual, my thoughts
began to wander. I had to will
myself to see what I was seeing
and nothing else. I had to tell myself *this* is what
mattered, not the other. (And I did see it,
for a minute or two!) For a minute or two
it crowded out the usual musings on
what was right, and what was wrong—duty,
tender memories, thoughts of death, how I should treat
with my former wife. All the things
I hoped would go away this morning.
The stuff I live with every day. What
I've trampled on in order to stay alive.

But for a minute or two I did forget
myself and everything else. I know I did.
For when I turned back I didn't know
where I was. Until some birds rose up
from the gnarled trees. And flew
in the direction I needed to be going.

8

ON THE AVENUE

20

Lawrence Ferlinghetti

The pennycandystore beyond the El
is where I first
            fell in love
                   with unreality
Jellybeans glowed in the semi-gloom
of that september afternoon
A cat upon the counter moved among
                  the licorice sticks
        and tootsie rolls
      and Oh Boy Gum

Outside the leaves were falling as they died

A wind had blown away the sun

A girl ran in
Her hair was rainy
Her breasts were breathless in the little room

Outside the leaves were falling
              and they cried
                    Too soon! too soon!

Shopping

Faith Shearin

My husband and I stood together in the new mall
which was clean and white and full of possibility.
We were poor so we liked to walk through the stores
since this was like walking through our dreams.
In one we admired coffee makers, blue pottery
bowls, toaster ovens as big as televisions. In another,

we eased into a leather couch and imagined
cocktails in a room overlooking the sea. When we
sniffed scented candles we saw our future faces,
softly lit, over a dinner of pasta and wine. When
we touched thick bathrobes we saw midnight

swims and bathtubs so vast they might be
mistaken for lakes. My husband's glasses hurt
his face and his shoes were full of holes.
There was a space in our living room where
a couch should have been. We longed for

fancy shower curtains, flannel sheets,
shiny silverware, expensive winter coats.
Sometimes, at night, we sat up and made lists.
We pressed our heads together and wrote
our wants all over torn notebook pages.
Nearly everyone we loved was alive and we

were in love but we liked wanting. Nothing
was ever as nice when we brought it home.
The objects in stores looked best in stores.
The stores were possible futures and, young
and poor, we went shopping. It was nice
then: we didn't know we already had everything.

Eddie Priest's Barbershop & Notary

Closed Mondays

Kevin Young

is music   is men
off early from work   is waiting
for the chance at the chair
while the eagle claws holes
in your pockets   keeping
time   by the turning
of rusty fans   steel flowers with
cold breezes   is having nothing
better to do   than guess at the years
of hair   matted beneath the soiled caps
of drunks   the pain of running
a fisted comb through stubborn
knots   is the dark dirty low
down blues   the tender heads
of sons fresh from cornrows   all
wonder at losing   half their height
is a mother gathering hair   for good
luck   for a soft wig   is the round
difficulty of ears   the peach
faced boys asking Eddie
to cut in parts and arrows
wanting to have their names read
for just a few days   and among thin
jazz   is the quick brush of a done
head   and the black flood around
your feet   the grandfathers

stopping their games of ivory
dominoes   just before they reach the bone
yard   is winking widowers announcing
cut it clean off   I'm through courting
and hair only gets in the way   is the final
spin of the chair   a reflection of
a reflection   that sting of wintergreen
tonic   on the neck of a sleeping snow
haired man   when you realize it is
your turn   you are next

Un Bel Di

Gerald Locklin

Because my daughter's eighth-grade teachers
Are having what is called an "in-service day,"
Which means, in fact, an out-of-service day,

She is spending this Friday home with me,
So I get up in time to take us,
On this summery day in March,
For a light lunch at a legendary café
Near the Yacht Marina.

Then we feed some ducks before catching
The cheap early-bird showing of
My Cousin Vinny, at which we share a
Dessert of a box of Milk Duds large
Enough to last us the entire show.

Afterwards we drive to a shoe-store to
Get her the Birkenstocks she's been coveting,

But they're out of her size in green; we leave
An order and stop for dinner at Norm Calvin's
Texas-style hole-in-the-wall barbeque rib factory.

When we get home I am smart enough
To downplay to my wife what a good day

We have had on our own. Later, saying
Goodnight to my little girl,

Already much taller than her mother,
I say, "days like today are the favorite
Days of my life," and she knows

It is true.

Beans and Franks

Donald Hall

When Newberry's closed
in Franklin, New Hampshire—homely lime front
    on Main Street, among the closed
storefronts of this mill town depressed
    since nineteen twenty-nine;
with its lunch counter for beans and franks
    and coleslaw; with its

bins of peanuts, counters of acrylic,
    hair nets, underwear, workshirts,
marbled notebooks, Bic pens, plastic
    toys, and cheap sneakers;
where Marjorie worked ten years at the iron
    cash register, Alcibide
Monbouquet pushed a broom at night.
    and Mr. Smith managed—
we learned that a man from Beverly
    Hills owned it, who never saw
the streets of Franklin, New Hampshire,
    and drew with a well-groomed hand
a line through "Franklin, New Hampshire."

At the Town Dump

Jane Kenyon

Sometimes I nod to my neighbor
as he flings lath and plaster or cleared
brush on the swelling pile. Talk
is impossible; the dozer shudders toward us,
flattening everything in its path.

Last March I got stuck in the mud.
Archie Portigue was there, thin
from the cancer that would kill him,
with his yellow pickup, its sides
akimbo from many loads. Archie
pushed as I rocked the car; the clutch
smelled hot; then with finesse
he jumped on the fender. . . . Saved,
I saw his small body in the rearview mirror
get smaller as he waved.

A boy pokes with a stick at a burnt-out
sofa cushion. . . . He brings the insides
out with clear delight. Near where I stand
the toe of a boot protrudes from the sand.

Today I brought the bug-riddled remains
of my garden. A single ripe tomato—last fruit,
immaculate—evaded harvest, and dangles
from a vine. I offer it to oblivion
with the rest of what was mine.

The Elopement

Sharon Olds

It was raining upwards, sideways, each
tree bursting with rain like brilliant
sweat. We stopped at a country store
to ask where we could get married. There were vats
of pickles, barrels of square yellow crackers,
the Prop. gave us the local J. P.'s
number. It was gently misting, in there,
brine and cracker-salt. The J. P. asked
if we'd get married in his church. While he called his minister
I wandered, in the dark, store
air, past the columns of vertebrate tin.
The shelves, and floor, and counters were old
wood, there must have been mice in the building,
rats, a cat, roaches, beetles,
and, in the barrel, whatever makes water
pickle, the mother of vinegar, it was
a spore Eden, a bestiary,
the minister said Yes, come right on over,
but maybe we had been married, there,
by matter, by the pickles, by the crackers, by the balls
of guard-fur, the rats looking away
into the long reaches, like the cows
in the manger, by the creche, though there's always one
who widens her glowing eyes, and gazes—one
rat, transfixed by mortal coupling
grabbed the Dutch Girl cocoa tin in his
arms and spun her in a dervish mazurka,

then all the witnesses waltzed, the Campbell's-soup
twins, the Gerber baby, Aunt
Jemima, Betty Crocker, the Sun Maid
raisin girl, the oats Quaker,
the chef of Cream of Wheat, every
good, mild, family guest
danced at our marriage, cloudy ions in the
cucumber-barrel spiraled, our eggs and
sperm swam in tandem, in water-
ballet, the spores of the sky whirled and
kissed on our wedding day.

I Ride Greyhound

Ellie Schoenfeld

because it's like being
in a John Steinbeck novel.
Next best thing is the laundromat.
That's where all people
who would be on the bus if they had the money
hang out. This is my crowd.
Tonight there are cleaning people appalled
at the stupidity of anyone
who would put powder detergent
into the clearly marked LIQUID ONLY slot.
The couple by the vending machine
are fondling each other.
You'd think the orange walls
and fluorescent lights
would dampen that energy
but it doesn't seem to.
It's a singles scene here on Saturday nights.
I confide to the fellow next to me
that I suspect I am being taken
in by the triple loader,
maybe it doesn't hold any more
than the regular machines
but I'm paying an extra fifty cents.
I tell him this meaningfully
holding handfuls of underwear.
He claims the triple loader
gives a better wash.

I don't ask why,
just cruise over to the pop machine,
aware that my selection
may provide a subtle clue.
I choose Wild Berry,
head back to my clothes.

Coffee Cup Café

Linda M. Hasselstrom

Soon as the morning chores are done,
cows milked, pigs fed, kids packed
off to school, it's down to the café
for more coffee and some soothing
conversation.

"If it don't rain pretty soon, I'm
just gonna dry up and blow away."

"Dry? This ain't dry. You don't know
how bad it can get. Why, in the Thirties
it didn't rain any more than this for
(breathless pause)   six years."

"I heard Johnson's lost ninety head of calves
in that spring snowstorm. They
were calving and heading for home
at the same time and they just walked
away from them."

"Yeah and when the cows
got home, half of them died
of pneumonia."

"I ain't had any hay on me since that hail
last summer; wiped out my hay crop, all

my winter pasture, and then the drouth
this spring. Don't know what I'll do."

"Yeah, but this is nothing yet.
Why in the Thirties the grasshoppers came
like hail and left nothing green on the ground.
They ate fenceposts, even. And the dust, why
it was deep as last winter's snow drifts,
piled against the houses. It ain't bad here yet,
and when it does come, there won't be so many of us
having coffee."

So for an hour they cheer each other, each story
worse than the last, each face longer. You'd think
they'd throw themselves under their tractors
when they leave, but they're bouncy as a new calf,
caps tilted fiercely into the sun.

They feel better, now they know
somebody's having a harder time
and that men like them
can take it.

The Ineffable

George Bilgere

I'm sitting here reading the paper,
feeling warm and satisfied, basically content
with my life and all I have achieved.
Then I go up for a refill and suddenly realize
how much happier I could be with the barista.
Late thirties, hennaed hair, an ankh
or something tattooed on her ankle,
a little silver ring in her nostril.
There's some mystery surrounding why she's here,
pouring coffee and toasting bagels at her age.
But there's a lot of torsion when she walks,
which is interesting. I can sense right away
how it would all work out between us.

We'd get a loft in the artsy part of town,
and I can see how we'd look shopping together
at our favorite organic market
on a snowy winter Saturday,
snowflakes in our hair,
our arms full of leeks and shiitake mushrooms.
We would do *tai chi* in the park.
She'd be one of the few people
who actually "gets" my poetry
which I'd read to her in bed.
And I can see us making love, by candlelight,
Struggling to find words for the ineffable.
We never dreamed it could be like this.

And it would all be great, for many months,
until one day, unable to help myself,
I'd say something about that nostril ring.
Like, do you really need to wear that tonight
at Sarah and Mike's house, Sarah and Mike being
pediatricians who intimidate me slightly
with their patrician cool, and serious money.
And she would give me a look,
a certain lifting of the eyebrows
I can see she's capable of, and right there
that would be the end of the ineffable.

People Who Eat in Coffee Shops

Edward Field

People who eat in coffee shops
are not worried about nutrition.
They order the toasted cheese sandwiches blithely,
followed by chocolate egg creams and plaster of paris
wedges of lemon meringue pie.
They don't have parental, dental, or medical figures hovering
full of warnings, or whip out dental floss immediately.
They can live in furnished rooms and whenever they want
go out and eat glazed donuts along with innumerable coffees,
dousing their cigarettes in sloppy saucers.

Ode to Hardware Stores

Barbara Hamby

Where have all the hardware stores gone—dusty, sixty-watt
    warrens with wood floors, cracked linoleum,
poured concrete painted blood red? Where are Eppes, Terry Rosa,
    Yon's, Flint—low buildings on South Monroe,
Eighth Avenue, Gaines Street with their scent of paint thinner,
    pesticides, plastic hoses coiled like serpents
in a garden paradisal with screws in buckets or bins
    against a brick wall with hand-lettered signs
in ball-point pen—*Carriage screws, two dozen for fifty cents*—
    long vicious dry-wall screws, thick wood screws
like peasants digging potatoes in fields, thin elegant trim
    screws—New York dames at a backwoods hick
Sunday School picnic. O universal clevis pins, seven holes
    in the shank, like the seven deadly sins.
Where are the men—Mr. Franks, Mr. Piggot, Tyrone, Hank,
    Ralph—sunburnt with stomachs and no asses,
men who knew the mythology of nails, Zeuses enthroned
    on an Olympus of weak coffee, bad haircuts,
and tin cans of galvanized casing nails, sinker nails, brads,
    20-penny common nails, duplex head nails, flooring nails
like railroad spikes, finish nails, fence staples, cotter pins,
    roofing nails—flat-headed as Floyd Crawford,
who lived next door to you for years but would never say hi
    or make eye contact. What a career in hardware
he could have had, his blue-black hair slicked back with
    brilliantine, rolling a toothpick between his teeth while sorting

screw eyes and carpet tacks. Where are the hardware stores,
    open Monday through Friday, Saturday till two?
No night hours here, like physicists their universe mathematical
    and pure in its way: dinner at six, *Rawhide* at eight,
lights out at ten, kiss in the dark, up at five for the subatomic world
    of toggle bolts, cap screws, hinch-pin clips, split-lock
washers. And the tools—saws, rakes, wrenches, rachets, drills,
    chisels, and hose heads, hose couplings, sandpaper
(garnet, production, wet or dry), hinges, wire nails, caulk, nuts, lag
    screws, pulleys, vise grips, hexbolts, fender washers,
all in a primordial stew of laconic talk about football, baseball,
    who'll start for the Dodgers, St. Louis, the Phillies,
the Cubs? Walk around the block today and see their ghosts:
    abandoned lots, graffitti'd windows, and tacked
to backroom walls, pin-up calendars almost decorous
    in our porn-riddled galaxy of Walmarts, Seven-Elevens,
stripmalls like strip mines or a carrion bird's curved beak
    gobbling farms, meadows, wildflowers, drowsy afternoons
of nothing to do but watch dust motes dance through a streak
    of sunlight in a darkened room. If there's a second coming,
I want angels called Lem, Nelson, Rodney, and Cletis gathered
    around a bin of nails, their silence like hosannahs,
hallelujahs, amens swelling from cinderblock cathedrals
    drowning our cries of *Bigger, faster, more, more, more.*

I Heard You Solemn-Sweet Pipes of the Organ

Walt Whitman

I heard you solemn-sweet pipes of the organ as last Sunday
    morn I pass'd the church,
Winds of autumn, as I walk'd the woods at dusk I heard
    your long-stretch'd sighs up above so mournful,
I heard the perfect Italian tenor singing at the opera, I heard
    the soprano in the midst of the quartet singing;
Heart of my love! you too I heard murmuring low through
    one of the wrists around my head,
Heard the pulse of you when all was still ringing little bells
    last night under my ear.

On the Day of Jayne Mansfield's Death

Nancy Vieira Couto

he offers me a ride to the laundromat
in his white '59 Ford. We stop at Oscar's
to buy detergent. They bunch around the radio—
old Oscar, two women in housedresses
and anklesocks, and a cat that flicks its tail
to the static. Of course it's inconceivable
that it should happen, that we should hear the news
here in the Adirondacks, where nothing happens.

There is nobody else in the laundromat.
We stuff machines, measure out the Tide,
plunge quarters into boxes. He unrolls
his sleeves, removes his shirt and throws it in,
watches it disappear. We sit by the window
and talk about the trip he's just returned from.
Salinas, the labor camp. The whores
in Salt Lake City. Selling a pool cue
for gas money somewhere in Missouri.
I listen, hungry. I know he's only nineteen.
He's wearing the cleanest undershirt that I've ever seen.

Suddenly I'm spinning in a machine,
pelted with the centrifugal slap of mink,
sable, satin. Bras the size of spinnakers
tack across the far side of the Maytag.
My hair spools out with the blonde bounce of silk.
His muscles are bigger and shinier than Mickey Hargitay's.

To Mecca With Love

James Tracy

After work at H and M Market Liquor and Deli,
quietly pondering the choices life gives us—
a Twenty-First Century natural selection:

Coke or Pepsi
Seven-Up or Sprite
Dr. Pepper or Mr. Pibb
Old English or Guinness in a Can
Doritos or Encharitos
Lottery or Super-Lotto

Someone is haggling for a forty-ouncer.
Someone is scratching a lottery ticket.
Someone calls out for spare change.

Behind the canned food aisles,
underneath the glow of the far security monitor,
I hear a man chant, the one who sold me
last night's beer, chips and tuna.

He is chanting devotion to Allah,
to Mecca with Love,
crouched on a cardboard flat;
a lone tear rests on his cheek.

A poster of a blonde straddling a beer can hears
his prayers.

The hum of the freezer harmonizes with him tonight.
Someone is still haggling for a forty-ouncer.

I walk to the counter to the man
who will sell me
tonight's beer, chips and tuna.

He says, "How's it goin'?"
I say, "Pretty good, same as usual."
He says, "Anything else?"
I say, "Yeah, a newspaper."

Walking away I look at the front page headlines

BLOODSHED AS ISRAEL RETALIATES
IN WEST BANK: 13 DEAD.

Minor League Rainout, Iowa

Mark J. Mitchell

Even today—the sun gone missing,

sky solid, sodden, all over gray,
wind bursting umbrellas—today

I can remember everything:
the small ball park in Iowa,
young athletes in cheap caps waiting
for the wind to stop, rains to go away

so a game could start. The grounds crew
smoking by the tarp spool (a drain
pipe, really), calm, ready to do
their act. And brats on coals, hissing
as raindrops pop their casings. Blue-
white lightning in the south, playing
tag with the light towers. The huge
river swelling, rolling away.

Even today—must be the storm—
while we walked the wet streets we knew
the game was holy and the rain
was sacred. We turned chairs facing
the Travel Lodge window, got warm,
watched the rain, the river, the blue-
black streets. Strangers from out of state

transfixed by weather, just sitting,
looking as clouds and lightning formed
new toys for God. I looked at you,
though you didn't know: wet, wild, fey
as you looked at the sky, wishing

there were words for this. Now transformed
into memory, it comes back, new,
borne by a cold and rainy day.
Your eyes, your wet hair, our kissing.

The Court of the Two Sisters

Phillip Lopate

The slow green fans turning in the courtyard
Of the classy restaurant in New Orleans;
The green napkins and the Negro waiters
Advancing in their bright green uniforms, superiorly
Filling the large water goblets dusty in the sun.
The hot rolls with curled butter shells like snails
And the enormous breakfasts served at all hours
Of Eggs with lemon sauce, asparagus, ham and toast points;
Cold creamed shrimp soup, oranges.
I read two newspapers at once, starting with sports;
Crowding the tablecloth with unwanted sections.
And when I was too stuffed to go on
I ordered a chickory coffee, dark and bitter
And a Charlotte Russe bursting with whipped cream.

I Went into the Maverick Bar

Gary Snyder

I went into the Maverick Bar
In Farmington, New Mexico.
And drank double shots of bourbon
               backed with beer.
My long hair was tucked up under a cap
I'd left the earring in the car.

Two cowboys did horseplay
               by the pool tables,
A waitress asked us
               where are you from?
a country-and-western band began to play
"We don't smoke Marijuana in Muskokie"
And with the next song,
               a couple began to dance.

They held each other like in High School dances
               in the fifties;
I recalled when I worked in the woods
               and the bars of Madras, Oregon.
That short-haired joy and roughness—
               America—your stupidity.
I could almost love you again.

We left—onto the freeway shoulders—
                under the tough old stars—
In the shadow of bluffs
                I came back to myself,
To the real work, to
                "What is to be done."

American Triptych

Jane Kenyon

1 AT THE STORE

Clumps of daffodils along the storefront
bend low this morning, late snow
pushing their bright heads down.
The flag snaps and tugs at the pole
beside the door.

The old freezer, full of Maine blueberries
and breaded scallops, mumbles along.
A box of fresh bananas on the floor,
luminous and exotic. . . .
I take what I need from the narrow aisles.

Cousins arrive like themes and variations.
Ansel leans on the counter,
remembering other late spring snows,
the blue snow of '32:
Yes, it *was*, it was *blue*.
Forrest comes and goes quickly
with a length of stovepipe, telling
about the neighbors' chimney fire.

The store is a bandstand. All our voices
sound from it, making the same motley
American music Ives heard;
this piece starting quietly,

with the repeated clink of a flagpole
pulley in the doorway of a country store.

2 DOWN THE ROAD

Early summer. Sun low over the pond. Down the road the neighbors' children play baseball in the twilight. I see the ball leave the bat; a moment later the sound reaches me where I sit.

No deaths or separations, no disappointments in love. They are throwing and hitting the ball. Sometimes it arcs higher than the house, sometimes it tunnels into tall grass at the edge of the hayfield.

3 POTLUCK AT THE WILMOT FLAT BAPTIST CHURCH

We drive to the Flat on a clear November night. Stars and planets appear in the eastern sky, not yet in the west.

Voices rise from the social hall downstairs, the clink of silverware and plates, the smell of coffee.

As we walk into the room faces turn to us, friendly and curious. We are seated at the speakers' table, next to the town historian, a retired schoolteacher who is lively and precise.

The table is decorated with red, white, and blue streamers, and framed *Time* and *Newsweek* covers of the President, just elected. Someone has tied peanuts to small branches with red, white, and blue yarn, and set the branches upright in lumps of clay at the center of each table.

After the meal everyone clears food from the tables, and tables from the hall. Then we go up to the sanctuary, where my husband reads poems from the pulpit.

One woman looks out the window continually. I notice the altar cloth, tasseled and embroidered in gold thread: Till I Come. There is applause after each poem.

On the way home we pass the white clapboard faces of the library and town hall, luminous in the moonlight, and I remember the first time I ever voted—in a township hall in Michigan.

That same wonderful smell of coffee was in the air, and I found myself among people trying to live ordered lives. . . . And again I am struck with love for the Republic.

9

SNOW

Snow: I

C.K. Williams

All night, snow, then, near dawn, freezing rain, so that by morning
      the whole city glistens
in a glaze of high-pitched, meticulously polished brilliance,
      everything rounded off,
the cars submerged nearly to their windows in the unbroken drifts
      lining the narrow alleys,
the buildings rising from the trunklike integuments the wind has
      molded against them.
Underlit clouds, blurred, violet bars, the rearguard of the storm,
      still hang in the east,
immobile over the flat river basin of the Delaware; beyond them,
      nothing, the washed sky,
one vivid wisp of pale smoke rising waveringly but emphatically
      into the brilliant ether.
No one is out yet but Catherine, who closes the door behind her
      and starts up the street.

Bright Sun after Heavy Snow

Jane Kenyon

A ledge of ice slides from the eaves,
piercing the crusted drift. Astonishing
how even a little violence
eases the mind.

In this extreme state of light
everything seems flawed: the streaked
pane, the forced bulbs on the sill
that refuse to bloom. . . . A wad of dust
rolls like a desert weed
over the drafty floor.

Again I recall a neighbor's
small affront—it rises in my mind
like the huge banks of snow along the road:
the plow, passing up and down all day,
pushes them higher and higher. . . .

The shadow of smoke rising from the chimney
moves abruptly over the yard.
The clothesline rises in the wind. One
wooden pin is left, solitary as a finger;
it, too, rises and falls.

The Snowbound City

John Haines

I believe in this stalled magnificence,
this churning chaos of traffic,
a beast with broken spine,
its hoarse voice hooded in feathers
and mist; the baffled eyes
wink amber and slowly darken.

Of men and women suddenly walking,
stumbling with little sleighs
in search of Tibetan houses—
dust from a far-off mountain
already whitens their shoulders.

When evening falls in blurred heaps,
a man losing his way among churches
and schoolyards feels under his cold hand
the stone thoughts of that city,

impassable to all but a few children
who went on into the hidden life
of caves and winter fires,
their faces glowing with disaster.

Snow, Aldo

Kate DiCamillo

Once, I was in New York,
in Central Park, and I saw
an old man in a black overcoat walking
a black dog. This was springtime
and the trees were still
bare and the sky was
gray and low and it began, suddenly,
to snow:
big fat flakes
that twirled and landed on the
black of the man's overcoat and
the black dog's fur. The dog
lifted his face and stared
up at the sky. The man looked
up, too. "Snow, Aldo," he said to the dog,
"snow." And he laughed.
The dog looked
at him and wagged his tail.

If I was in charge of making
snow globes, this is what I would put inside:
the old man in the black overcoat,
the black dog,
two friends with their faces turned up to the sky

as if they were receiving a blessing,
as if they were being blessed together
by something
as simple as snow
in March.

Winter Afternoon

Grace Paley

Old men and women walk by my window
they're frightened   it's icy wintertime
they take small steps   they're looking
at their feet   they're glad to be
going   they hate
the necessity

sometimes the women wear heels   why
do they do this   the old women's
heads are bent   they see their shoes
which are often pointy   these shoes
were made for crossed legs in the
evening   pointing

                              sometimes the old men
walk a dog   the dog moves too fast
the man stands still   the dog stands
still   the smells come to the dog
floating from the square earth of the
plane tree   from the tires of cars
at rest   all this interesting life
and adventure comes to the waiting dog
the man doesn't know this   the street
is too icy   old women in pointy shoes
and high heels pass him   their necks
in fur collars bent   their eyes watch
their small slippery feet

The Legend

Garrett Hongo

In Chicago, it is snowing softly
and a man has just done his wash for the week.
He steps into the twilight of early evening,
carrying a wrinkled shopping bag
full of neatly folded clothes,
and, for a moment, enjoys
the feel of warm laundry and crinkled paper,
flannellike against his gloveless hands.
There's a Rembrandt glow on his face,
a triangle of orange in the hollow of his cheek
as a last flash of sunset
blazes the storefronts and lit windows of the street.

He is Asian, Thai or Vietnamese,
and very skinny, dressed as one of the poor
in rumpled suit pants and a plaid mackinaw,
dingy and too large.
He negotiates the slick of ice
on the sidewalk by his car,
opens the Fairlane's back door,
leans to place the laundry in,
and turns, for an instant,
toward the flurry of footsteps
and cries of pedestrians
as a boy—that's all he was—
backs from the corner package store
shooting a pistol, firing it,

once, at the dumbfounded man
who falls forward,
grabbing his chest.

A few sounds escape from his mouth,
a babbling no one understands
as people surround him
bewildered at his speech.
The noises he makes are nothing to them.
The boy has gone, lost
in the light array of foot traffic
dappling the snow with fresh prints.

Tonight, I read about Descartes'
grand courage to doubt everything
except his own miraculous existence
and I feel so distinct
from the wounded man lying on the concrete
I am ashamed.

Let the night sky cover him as he dies.
Let the weaver girl cross the bridge of heaven
and take up his cold hands.

Snowbound

David Tucker

The runways were covered by early evening,
nothing moved out there but the occasional noble
snowplow carrying on with a yellow grimace;
the jet fleets were barely visible, like whales
sleeping off the blast. The concourses, so frantic
a few hours ago, were almost still; a few meanderers chatted
on their cell phones and looked at watches. Some
who couldn't bear the limbo lined up at the ticket counters
to argue with clerks who rolled their eyes.
Expectations that could not be denied on this
of all days were denied, deadlines that couldn't be missed
were missed, helpless executives threw up their hands,
meetings went on without them, soldiers with orders
gave up with good cheer and played video games
as if this were finally the last place and not all that bad,
stranded students slept on backpacks, wedding guests
rode the escalators with vacant stares, imagining the bride.
I stayed quiet and thought of you, checked my passport and
    my ticket,
like a spy with only a name to get me out,
a thousand miles from my life.

Manna

Joseph Stroud

Everywhere, *everywhere*, snow sifting down,
a world becoming white, no more sounds,
no longer possible to find the heart of the day,
the sun is gone, the sky is nowhere, and of all
I wanted in life—so be it—whatever it is
that brought me here, chance, fortune, whatever
blessing each flake of snow is the hint of, I am
grateful, I bear witness, I hold out my arms,
palms up, I know it is impossible to hold
for long what we love of the world, but look
at me, is it foolish, shameful, arrogant to say this,
see how the snow drifts down, look how happy
I am.

Outside of Richmond, Virginia, Sunday

Deborah Slicer

It's the kind of mid-January afternoon—
the sky as calm as an empty bed,
fields indulgent,
black Angus finally sitting down to chew—
that makes a girl ride her bike up and down the same
     muddy track of road
between the gray barn and the state highway
all afternoon, the black mutt
with the white patch like a slap on his rump
loping after the rear tire, so happy.
Right after Sunday dinner
until she can see the headlights out on the dark highway,
she rides as though she has an understanding with the track she's
     opened up in the road,
with the two wheels that slide and stutter in the red mud
but don't run off from under her,
with the dog who knows to stay out of the way but to stay.
And even after the winter cold draws tears,
makes her nose run,
even after both sleeves are used up,
she thinks a life couldn't be any better than this.
And hers won't be,
and it will be very good.

The Snowstorm

Ralph Waldo Emerson

Announced by all the trumpets of the sky,
Arrives the snow, and, driving o'er the fields,
Seems nowhere to alight: the whited air
Hides hills and woods, the river, and the heaven,
And veils the farm-house at the garden's end.
The sled and traveller stopped, the courier's feet
Delayed, all friends shut out, the housemates sit
Around the radiant fireplace, enclosed
In a tumultuous privacy of storm.

Come see the north wind's masonry.
Out of an unseen quarry evermore
Furnished with tile, the fierce artificer
Curves his white bastions with projected roof
Round every windward stake, or tree, or door.
Speeding, the myriad-handed, his wild work
So fanciful, so savage, nought cares he
For number or proportion. Mockingly,
On coop or kennel he hangs Parian wreaths;
A swan-like form invests the hidden thorn;
Fills up the farmer's lane from wall to wall,
Maugre the farmer's sighs; and at the gate
A tapering turret overtops the work.
And when his hours are numbered,
      and the world

Is all his own, retiring, as he were not,
Leaves, when the sun appears, astonished Art
To mimic in slow structures, stone by stone,
Built in an age, the mad wind's night-work,
The frolic architecture of the snow.

A Pair of Barn Owls, Hunting

David Wagoner

Now slowly, smoothly flying over the field
Beside the orchard into the after-light
Of the cold evening, the ash gold owls come sailing
Close to the branches, gliding across the arbor
Where the bare grapevines ripen only shadows
In the dead of winter, and at the end of a garden
Suddenly flare their wings, hover,
And swerve, claws first, down to the grass together.

When I First Saw Snow

Tarrytown, N.Y.

Gregory Djanikian

Bing Crosby was singing "White Christmas"
    on the radio, we were staying at my aunt's house
    waiting for papers, my father was looking for a job.
We had trimmed the tree the night before,
    sap had run on my fingers and for the first time
    I was smelling pine wherever I went.
Anais, my cousin, was upstairs in her room
    listening to Danny and the Juniors.
Haigo was playing Monopoly with Lucy, his sister,
    Buzzy, the boy next door, had eyes for her
    and there was a rattle of dice, a shuffling
    of Boardwalk, Park Place, Marvin Gardens.
There were red bows on the Christmas tree.
It had snowed all night.
My boot buckles were clinking like small bells
    as I thumped to the door and out
    onto the grey planks of the porch dusted with snow.
The world was immaculate, new,
    even the trees had changed color,
    and when I touched the snow on the railing
    I didn't know what I had touched, ice or fire.
I heard, "I'm dreaming . . ."
I heard, "At the hop, hop, hop . . . oh, baby."
I heard "B & O" and the train in my imagination
    was whistling through the great plains.
And I was stepping off,
I was falling deeply into America.

Snow

Kenneth Rexroth

Low clouds hang on the mountain.
The forest is filled with fog.
A short distance away the
Giant trees recede and grow
Dim. Two hundred paces and
They are invisible. All
Day the fog curdles and drifts.
The cries of the birds are loud.
They sound frightened and cold. Hour
By hour it grows colder.
Just before sunset the clouds
Drop down the mountainside. Long
Shreds and tatters of fog flow
Swiftly away between the
Trees. Now the valley below
Is filled with clouds like clotted
Cream and over them the sun
Sets, yellow in a sky full
Of purple feathers. After dark
A wind rises and breaks branches
From the trees and howls in the
Treetops and then suddenly
Is still. Late at night I wake
And look out of the tent. The
Clouds are rushing across the
Sky and through them is tumbling
The thin waning moon. Later

All is quiet except for
A faint whispering. I look
Out. Great flakes of wet snow are
Falling. Snowflakes are falling
Into the dark flames of the
Dying fire. In the morning the
Pine boughs are sagging with snow,
And the dogwood blossoms are
Frozen, and the tender young
Purple and citron oak leaves.

I Want to Say

Natalie Goldberg

Before I'm lost to time and the midwest
I want to say I was here
I loved the half light all winter
I want you to know before I leave
that I liked the towns living along the back of the Mississippi
I loved the large heron filling the sky
the slender white egret at the edge of the shore
I came to love my life here
fell in love with the color grey
the unending turn of seasons

Let me say
I loved Hill City
the bench in front of the tavern
the small hill to the lake
I loved the morning frost on the bell in New Albin
and the money I made as a poet
I was thankful for the white night
the sky of so many wet summers
Before I leave this whole world of my friends
I want to tell you I loved the rain on large store windows
had more croissants here in Minneapolis
than the French do in Lyons
I read the poets of the midwest
their hard crusts of bread dark goat cheese
and was nourished not hungry where they lived
I ate at the edges of state lines and boundaries

Know I loved the cold the tap of bare branches against windows
know there will not be your peonies in spring
wherever I go
the electric petunias
and your orange zinnias

Upon Discovering My Entire Solution to the Attainment of Immortality Erased from the Blackboard Except the Word 'Save'

Dobby Gibson

If you have seen the snow
somewhere slowly fall
on a bicycle,
then you understand
all beauty will be lost
and that even that loss
can be beautiful.
And if you have looked
at a winter garden
and seen not a winter garden
but a meditation on shape,
then you know why
this season is not
known for its words,
the cold too much
about the slowing of matter,
not enough about the making of it.
So you are blessed
to forget this way:
a jump rope in the ice melt,
a mitten that has lost its hand,

a sun that shines
as if it doesn't mean it.
And if in another season
you see a beautiful woman
use her bare hands
to smooth wrinkles
from her expensive dress
for the sake of dignity,
but in so doing trace
the outlines of her thighs,
then you will remember
surprise assumes a space
that has first been forgotten,
especially here, where we
rarely speak of it,
where we walk out onto the roofs
of frozen lakes
simply because we're stunned
we really can.

Snow

Debra Nystrom

for Brad

Fifteen below and wind at sixty,
no way to get the feeder to the cattle;
they'll have to tough it out or not
till the gusting dies down—
if they weren't the neighbor's herd left
in your care you'd forget them—
no, they'd be gone, sold for the pleading
or the settlement, like everything;
you think of cutting the motor off to sit
in the tractor cab awhile, radio songs slowly
fading out as they suck the battery dry,
white nonsense scattering at the windshield
like bits of wreckage hypnotizing
till some kind of sleep comes on—
no sleeping in the house, the bedroom closed,
the kids' rooms too, you only go
to the couch and listen to television voices
calling as if to a lifeboat they don't
know anything about; once in a while the
answering machine—not her, just
your mother or sister, worried, trying to
coax you to the phone, draw you out,
but you're too tired to tell them there's
nothing left here to worry about:
if the gusting doesn't die down soon
the cold will finish all of it.

Snow-Flakes

Henry Wadsworth Longfellow

Out of the bosom of the Air,
　Out of the cloud-folds of her garments shaken,
Over the woodlands brown and bare,
　Over the harvest-fields forsaken,
　　Silent, and soft, and slow
　　Descends the snow.
Even as our cloudy fancies take
　Suddenly shape in some divine expression,
Even as the troubled heart doth make
　In the white countenance confession,
　　The troubled sky reveals
　　The grief it feels.
This is the poem of the air,
　Slowly in silent syllables recorded;
This is the secret of despair,
　Long in its cloudy bosom hoarded,
　　Now whispered and revealed
　　To wood and field.

10

RESIDENTIAL

Where I Live

Maxine Kumin

is vertical:
garden, pond, uphill

pasture, run-in shed.
Through pines, Pumpkin Ridge.

Two switchbacks down
church spire, spit of town.

Where I climb I inspect
the peas, cadets erect

in lime-capped rows,
hear hammer blows

as pileateds peck
the rot of shagbark hickories

enlarging last
year's pterodactyl nests.

Granite erratics
humped like bears

dot the outermost pasture
where in tall grass

clots of ovoid scat
butternut-size, milky brown

announce our halfgrown
moose padded past

into the forest
to nibble beech tree sprouts.

Wake-robin trillium
in dapple-shade. Violets,

landlocked seas I swim in.
I used to pick bouquets

for her, framed them
with leaves. *Schmutzige*

she said, holding me close
to scrub my streaky face.

Almost from here I touch
my mother's death.

Fields

Faith Shearin

For Henry and Irene Spruill

My great grandfather had some fields in North Carolina
and he willed those fields to his sons and his sons
willed them to their sons so there is a two-hundred-year-old
farm house on that land where several generations
of my family fried chicken and laughed and hung

their laundry beneath the trees. There are things you
know when your family has lived close to the earth:
things that make magic seem likely. Dig a hole on the new
of the moon and you will have dirt to throw away
but dig one on the old of the moon and you won't have

enough to fill it back up again: I learned this trick
in the backyard of childhood with my hands. If you know
the way the moon pulls at everything then you can feel
it on the streets of a city where you cannot see the sky.
My mother says the moon is like a man: it changes

its mind every eight days and you plant nothing
until it's risen full and high. If you plant corn when
the signs are in the heart you will get black spots
in your grain and if you meet a lover when the
signs are in the feet he will never take you dancing.

When the signs are in the bowels you must not plant
or your seed will rot and if you want to make a baby
you must undress under earth or water. I am the one

in the post office who buys stamps when the signs
are in air so my mail will learn to fly. I stand in my

front yard, in the suburbs, and wish for luck and
money on the new of the moon when there
are many black nights. I may walk the streets
of this century and make my living in an office
but my blood is old farming blood and my true

self is underground like a potato. At the opera
I will think of rainfall and vines. In my dreams
all my corn may grow short but the ears will be
full. If you kiss my forehead on a dark moon
in March I may disappear—but do not be afraid—
I have taken root in my grandfather's
fields: I am hanging my laundry beneath his trees.

Monticello

May Sarton

This legendary house, this dear enchanted tomb,
Once so supremely lived in, and for life designed,
Will none of moldy death nor give it room,
Charged with the presence of a living mind.

Enter, and touch the temper of a lively man.
See, it is spacious, intimate, and full of light.
The eye, pleased by detail, is nourished by the plan;
Nothing is here for show, much for delight.

All the joys of invention and of craft and wit,
Are freely granted here, all given rein,
But taut within the classic form and ruled by it,
Elegant, various, magnificent—and plain,

Europe become implacably American!
Yet Mozart could have been as happy here,
As Monroe riding from his farm again,
As well as any silversmith or carpenter—

As well as we, for whom this elegance,
This freedom in a form, this peaceful grace,
Is not our heritage, although it happened once:
We read the future, not the past, upon his face.

Inheritance

W. S. Merwin

At my elbow on the table
it lies open as it has done
for a good part of these thirty
years ever since my father died
and it passed into my hands
this *Webster's New International*
Dictionary of the English
Language of 1922
on India paper which I
was always forbidden to touch
for fear I would tear or somehow
damage its delicate pages
heavy in their binding
this color of wet sand
on which thin waves hover
when it was printed he was twenty-six
they had not been married four years
he was a country preacher
in a one-store town and I suppose
a man came to the door one day
peddling this new dictionary
on fine paper like the Bible
at an unrepeatable price
and it seemed it would represent
a distinction just to own it
confirming something about him
that he could not even name

now its cover is worn as though
it had been carried on journeys
across the mountains and deserts
of the earth but it has been here
beside me the whole time
what has frayed it like that
loosening it gnawing at it
all through these years
I know I must have used it
much more than he did but always
with care and indeed affection
turning the pages patiently
in search of meanings

Unfortunate Location

Louis Jenkins

In the front yard there are three big white pines, older than any-thing in the neighborhood except the stones. Magnificent trees that toss their heads in the wind like the spirited black horses of a troika. It's hard to know what to do, tall dark trees on the south side of the house, an unfortunate location, blocking the winter sun. Dark and damp. Moss grows on the roof, the porch timbers rot and surely the roots have reached the old bluestone foundation. At night, in the wind, a tree could stumble and fall killing us in our beds. The needles fall year after year making an acid soil where no grass grows. We rake the fallen debris, nothing to be done, we stand around with sticks in our hands. Wonderful trees.

Sunday Dinner

Dan Masterson

Linen napkins, spotless from the wash, starched
And ironed, smelling like altar cloths. Olives
And radishes wet in cut glass, a steaming gravy bowl
Attached to its platter, an iridescent pitcher cold
With milk, the cream stirred in moments before.

The serving fork, black bone at the handle, capped
In steel, tines sharp as hatpins. Stuffed celery,
Cut in bite-sized bits, tomato juice flecked
With pepper, the vinegar cruet full to the stopper
Catching light from the chandelier.

Once-a-week corduroyed plates with yellow trim,
A huge mound of potatoes mashed and swirled.
Buttered corn, side salads topped with sliced tomatoes,
A tall stack of bread, a quarter-pound of butter
Warmed by its side. And chicken, falling off the bone:
Crisp skin baked sweet with ten-minute bastings.

Homemade pies, chocolate mints and puddings,
Coffee and graceful glasses of water, chipped ice
Clinking the rims.

Cashews in a silver scoop, the centerpiece a milkglass
Compote with caved-in sides, laced and hung
With grapes, apples, and oranges for the taking.

Eight. Doing the Dishes

Jeanne Lohmann

We lived in so many houses, Gloria: Indiana Avenue,
Summit and Fourth, the double on Hudson Street.
And that upstairs apartment on North High we rented
from Armbruster's. Mother thought it Elizabethan,
romantic, with its leaded glass windows and wood-beamed
ceilings. Our entrance was at the side, at the top of stairs
that creaked late at night when we came home from our dates.
You had more of these than I did, even if I was older.
It was 1943, and our brother Harry was in the Navy.
I'd had a year away at college, and you were
still in high school. On this particular night
in the kitchen, doing the supper dishes, you
drying while I washed, you told me that your friend
Monabelle had a premature baby, and you'd been there,
helped to find a shoebox to put the baby in. I tried
to imagine this, kept seeing the cardboard box
with the baby, Monabelle bleeding and crying.
You didn't want our parents to hear, so we talked
softly while we put the dishes in the drainer
on the sink and hung the towels to dry.
The pilot light on the range burned purple blue
and I saw both of us new in that light, you
with so much to teach me, my self-absorbed
studious life, so intent on saving the world.

Porches II

Virginia Hamilton Adair

All over our U.S. the porches were dying.
The porch swing and the rocking chair moved to the
    village dump.
The floorboards trembled, and the steps creaked.
For a couple of decades a new light burned in the parlor,
the family sitting there silent in front of the box,
voices and music squawking mysteriously from far places
into the dim-lit room. Conversation was hushed.

In the next two decades, a window in the box
flashed unbelievable pictures into the room.
Strangers guffawed and howled with laughter.
Shots rang out, people died in front of our eyes.
We learned not to care, drinking Coca-Cola from bottles,
spilling popcorn into the sofa.

A highway came past the house with its deserted porch
and no one noticed. The children wandered off to rob houses
a few blocks away, not out of need, but simple boredom.
No more family games or read-alouds.

Grandparents sometimes pulled their chairs outside
hoping neighbors would stop in.
They might even drag out an extra chair or two;
Still no one came, not even to borrow something.

But it was hard to talk with the TV at their backs,
the traffic screeching by in front, the rest of the neighborhood
on relief, or in rest homes and reformatories.

The old porch is removed, and the grandparents with it.
So long, friends, neighbors, passersby.

The Fat of the Land

Ronald Wallace

Gathered in the heavy heat of Indiana,
summer and 102°, we've come from
all over this great country,
one big happy family, back from
wherever we've spread ourselves too thin.
A cornucopia of cousins and uncles, grand-
parents and aunts, nieces and nephews, expanding.
All day we laze on the oily beach;
we eat all the smoke-filled evening:
shrimp dip and crackers,
Velveeta cheese and beer,
handfuls of junk food, vanishing.
We sit at card tables, examining
our pudgy hands, piling in
hot fudge and double chocolate
brownies, strawberry shortcake and cream,
as the lard-ball children
sluice from room to room.
O the loveliness of so much loved flesh,
the litany of split seams and puffed sleeves,
sack dresses and Sansabelt slacks,
dimpled knees and knuckles, the jiggle
of triple chins. O the gladness
that only a family understands,
our fat smiles dancing
as we play our cards right.
Our jovial conversation blooms and booms

in love's large company, as our sweet
words ripen and split their skins:
mulberry, fabulous, flotation,
phlegmatic, plumbaginous.
Let our large hearts attack us,
our blood run us off the scale.
We're huge and whole on this simmering night,
battened against the small skinny
futures that must befall all of us,
the gray thin days and the noncaloric dark.

Plastic Beatitude

Laure-Anne Bosselaar

Our neighbors, the Pazzottis, live in a long
narrow canary-yellow house with Mrs. Pazzotti's old
father, their 2 daughters, *their* husbands, 4 kids,
a tortoise shell cat and a white poodle.

Their yard is my childhood dream: toys,
bicycles, tubs, bird cages, barbecues, planters, pails, tools
and garden sculptures: an orange squirrel eating a nut,
Mickey Mouse pushing a wheelbarrow, St. Joseph
carrying a lantern, his other blessing hand
broken at the wrist, and two tea-sipping toads
in an S-shaped love seat, smiling at each other
under a polka-dotted parasol.

On the yellow railing around the deck,
a procession of nine pinwheels. This May morning,
they thrash the air with each breeze like clumsy angels
nailed to their posts. On the garage wall at the end of the
yard an electric cord shoots up to the roof. One half connects
to a blue neon insect electrocuter, the other half snakes to,
then disappears into a pedestal cemented on the cornice.

And there she stands, in plastic beatitude—and six feet
of it—the Madonna, in her white robe and blue cape, arms
outstretched, blessing the Pazzottis, their yard and neighbors,
lit from within day and night, calling God's little insects to
her shining light, before sending them straight

to the zapper—tiny buzzing heretics fried by the same
power that lured them to their last temptation.

Brothers and Sisters

Jim Harrison

I'm trying to open a window in this very old house of indeterminate age buried toward the back of a large ranch here in the Southwest, abandoned for so long that there's no road leading into it but a slight indentation in the pastureland, last lived in by the owner's great-uncle who moved to New York City to listen to music, or so he said, but his grandnephew said that the man was "light in his loafers," which was hard to be back in New Mexico in those days. In the pantry under a stained vinegar cruet is a sepia photo of him and his sister in their early teens on the front porch of the house, dressed unconvincingly as vaqueros, as handsome as young people get. The photo is dated 1927 and lights up the pantry. I find out that the girl died in childbirth in the middle thirties in Pasadena, the boy committed suicide in Havana in 1952, both dying in the hands of love. Out in the yard I shine my flashlight down a hole under a massive juniper stump. A rattlesnake forms itself into anxious coils surrounding its pretty babies stunned by the light.

227 Waverly Place

W.S. Merwin

When I have left I imagine they will
repair the window onto the fire escape
that looks north up the avenue clear
to Columbus Circle long I have known
the lights of that valley at every hour
through that unwashed pane and have watched with no
conclusion its river flowing toward me
straight from the featureless distance coming
closer darkening swelling growing distinct
speeding up as it passed below me toward
the tunnel all that time through all that time
taking itself through its sound which became
part of my own before long the unrolling
rumble the iron solos and the sirens
all subsiding in the small hours to voices
echoing from the sidewalks a rustling
in the rushes along banks and the loose
glass vibrated like a remembering bee
as the north wind slipped under the winter sill
at the small table by the window until
my right arm ached and stiffened and I pushed
the chair back against the bed and got up
and went out into the other room that was
filled with the east sky and the day replayed
from the windows and roofs of the Village
the room where friends came and we sat talking
and where we ate and lived together while

the blue paint flurried down from the ceiling
and we listened late with lights out to music
hearing the intercom from the hospital
across the avenue through the Mozart
Dr Kaplan wanted on the tenth floor
while reflected lights flowed backward on the walls

To His Piano

Howard Nemerov

Old friend, patient of error as of accuracy,
Ready to think the fingerings of thought,
You but a scant year older than I am
With my expectant mother expecting maybe
An infant prodigy among her stars
But getting only little me instead—

To see you standing there for six decades
Containing chopsticks, Fur Elise, and
The Art of Fugue in your burnished rosewood box,
As well as all those years of silence and
The stumbling beginnings the children made,
Who would believe the twenty tons of stress
Your gilded frame's kept stretched out all this while?

Letter Home

Ellen Steinbaum

I love you forever
my father's letter tells her
for forty-nine pages,
from the troopship crossing the Atlantic
before they'd ever heard of Anzio.

He misses her, the letter says,
counting out days of boredom, seasickness,
and changing weather,
poker games played for matches
when cash and cigarettes ran out,
a Red Cross package—soap,
cards, a mystery book he traded away
for *The Rubaiyyat* a bunkmate didn't want.
He stood night watch and thought
of her. Don't forget the payment
for insurance, he says.

My mother waits at home with me,
waits for the letter he writes day by day
moving farther across the ravenous ocean.
She will get it in three months and
her fingers will smooth the Army stationery
to suede.

He will come home, stand
beside her in the photograph, leaning

on crutches, holding
me against the rough wool
of his jacket. He will sit
alone and listen to *Aïda*

and they will pick up their
interrupted lives. Years later,
she will show her grandchildren
a yellow envelope with
forty-nine wilted pages telling her

of shimmering sequins on the water,
the moonlight catching sudden phosphorescence,
the churned wake that stretched a silver trail.

Crickets in the Dark

Tom Hennen

The farmhouse I'm staying in this year is a hundred years old, big, with six bedrooms upstairs and a walk-in attic. I sleep in the living room by the open bay windows where the scent of cow manure and lilacs floats in from around the turn of the century, a simpler time of flowers and dust. I am so far out on the prairie that there are no lights except mine, the stars', and the fireflies'. When my lights are off, only the stars and the fireflies are left to show the earth which way to turn, while in the darkness the crickets leap into the deep end of night, singing.

25th High School Reunion

Linda Pastan

We come to hear the endings
of all the stories
in our anthology
of false starts:
how the girl who seemed
as hard as nails
was hammered
into shape;
how the athletes ran
out of races;
how under the skin
our skulls rise
to the surface
like rocks in the bed
of a drying stream.
Look! We have all
turned into
ourselves.

11

GOOD WORK

The Zen of Mucking Out

Maxine Kumin

*I never liked this stubbled field so much
as now*, Keats wrote John Reynolds
and in my upper pasture I feel the same

where the last two horses of our lives
are at their day-long work reducing
the lightly frosted grass of mid-October

to manure, and I at mine, my five-
foot fork with ten metal tines, the hickory
handle worn down by my grip

so many years it almost seems to sweat—
muck basket to wheelbarrow, fork
upended till I reach the mother bed

and dump my smeary load, then stop.
White pine embroidery to the east,
a narrow view of Pumpkin Hill across,

lissome pond behind me. One late
garter snake sits sunning on an outcrop.
From the highway the vigor of sirens

announces a world of metal and speed
beyond my blinkered allegiance
to this task. My fingerprint,

my footstep. My zen.

"H"

Joyce Sutphen

Of all tractors, I love the "H" the best:
first for its proportions, the ratio of body to machine,
arm to wheel, leg to clutch, hand to throttle,

and for the way it does not drown the voice,
but forces it to rise above the engine,
and for the smoke signaling from the silver pipe,

for the rip-rap of tread on the big tires, driver
perched between them, as on a throne in kingdoms of oats
and corn, scrolling along the meadow's edge,

then sometimes standing still, engine turning the belt
that turned the wheels in the hammer mill
or whirling the gears that divided the oats from the straw.

And "H" for the ache to see my father plowing fields again—
the silhouette of a red tractor and a man, one hand
on the wheel, the other waving free.

After Work

Gary Snyder

The shack and a few trees
float in the blowing fog

I pull out your blouse,
warm my cold hands
    on your breasts.
you laugh and shudder
peeling garlic by the
    hot iron stove.
bring in the axe, the rake,
the wood

we'll lean on the wall
against each other
stew simmering on the fire
as it grows dark
    drinking wine.

Notes from the Delivery Room

Linda Pastan

Strapped down,
victim in an old comic book,
I have been here before,
this place where pain winces
off the walls
like too bright light.
Bear down a doctor says,
foreman to sweating laborer,
but this work, this forcing
of one life from another
is something that I signed for
at a moment when I would have signed anything.
Babies should grow in fields;
common as beets or turnips
they should be picked and held
root end up, soil spilling
from between their toes—
and how much easier it would be later,
returning them to earth.
Bear up . . . bear down . . . the audience
grows restive, and I'm a new magician
who can't produce the rabbit
from my swollen hat.
She's crowning, someone says,
but there is no one royal here,
just me, quite barefoot,
greeting my barefoot child.

Complaint

William Carlos Williams

They call me and I go.
It is a frozen road
past midnight, a dust
of snow caught
in the rigid wheeltracks.
The door opens.
I smile, enter and
shake off the cold.
Here is a great woman
on her side in the bed.
She is sick,
perhaps vomiting,
perhaps laboring
to give birth to
a tenth child. Joy! Joy!
Night is a room
darkened for lovers,
through the jalousies the sun
has sent one gold needle!
I pick the hair from her eyes
and watch her misery
with compassion.

Big Wind

Theodore Roethke

Where were the greenhouses going,
Lunging into the lashing
Wind driving water
So far down the river
All the faucets stopped?—
So we drained the manure-machine
For the steam plant,
Pumping the stale mixture
Into the rusty boilers,
Watching the pressure gauge
Waver over to red,
As the seams hissed
And the live steam
Drove to the far
End of the rose-house,
Where the worst wind was,
Creaking the cypress window-frames,
Cracking so much thin glass
We stayed all night,
Stuffing the holes with burlap;
But she rode it out,
That old rose-house,
She hove into the teeth of it,
The core and pith of that ugly storm,
Plowing with her stiff prow,
Bucking into the wind-waves
That broke over the hole of her,

Flailing her sides with spray,
Flinging long strings of wet across the rooftop,
Finally veering, wearing themselves out, merely
Whistling thinly under the wind-vents;
She sailed until the calm morning,
Carrying her full cargo of roses.

People Who Take Care

Nancy Henry

People who take care of people
get paid less than anybody
people who take care of people
are not worth much
except to people who are
sick, old, helpless, and poor
people who take care of people
are not important to most other people
are not respected by many other people
come and go without much fuss
unless they don't show up
when needed
people who make more money
tell them what to do
never get shit on their hands
never mop vomit or wipe tears
don't stand in danger
of having plates thrown at them
sharing every cold
observing agonies
they cannot tell at home
people who take care of people
have a secret
that sees them through the double shift
that moves with them from room to room
that keeps them on the floor

sometimes they fill a hollow
no one else can fill
sometimes through the shit
and blood and tears
they go to a beautiful place, somewhere
those clean important people
have never been.

Only What I Can Do

Julene Tripp Weaver

Dedicated to Juan Bernal, died September 9, 2001, at age 41

I write a letter for my client today.
I sit with him on the deck
of the skilled nursing facility.
He eats breakfast, smokes cigarettes.
He wants me to write to his baby brother
                              in jail doing time.
He dictates: *"I love you—*
I need a thousand dollars—
I will drive the get-away car."
He has these plans
he needs to convey—tells me
his little brother will tote the gun.

He dictates: *"The doctor told me today*
I am dying, but he doesn't know
how long it might take."

It is doubtful he will be able to drive
the get-away car when his legs are paralyzed
and two people have to transfer him
from his bed to his wheelchair and back.
He has a direct line morphine drip
he presses every ten minutes.

It is doubtful he will make it
home again, but he wants to go home.

He drifts in and out of sleep, nodding-out
his thoughts stop in mid-sentence,
he loses track of his message to his brother.

He asks if they'll read his letter.
The jail will, I say. He edits out the question
about whether his brother killed someone.
He thinks he did. I suggest he
take out the part about robbing a bank
but he doesn't. He thinks it's a good plan.

Wild Geese

Charles Goodrich

I'm picking beans when the geese fly over, Blue Lake pole beans I figure to blanch and freeze. Maybe pickle some dilly beans. And there will be more beans to give to the neighbors, forcibly if necessary.

The geese come over so low I can hear their wings creak, can see their tail feathers making fine adjustments. They slip-stream along so gracefully, riding on each other's wind, surfing the sky. Maybe after the harvest I'll head south. Somebody told me Puerto Vallarta is nice. I'd be happy with a cheap room. Rice and beans at every meal. Swim a little, lay on the beach.

Who are you kidding, Charles? You don't like to leave home in the winter. Spring, fall, or summer either. True. But I do love to watch those wild geese fly over, feel these impertinent desires glide through me. Then get back to work.

And One for My Dame

Anne Sexton

A born salesman,
my father made all his dough
by selling wool to Fieldcrest, Woolrich and Faribo.

A born talker,
he could sell one hundred wet-down bales
of that white stuff. He could clock the miles and sales

and make it pay.
At home each sentence he would utter
had first pleased the buyer who'd paid him off in butter.

Each word
had been tried over and over, at any rate,
on the man who was sold by the man who filled my plate.

My father hovered
over the Yorkshire pudding and the beef:
a peddler, a hawker, a merchant and an Indian chief.

Roosevelt! Willkie! and war!
How suddenly gauche I was
with my old-maid heart and my funny teenage applause.

Each night at home
my father was in love with maps
while the radio fought its battles with Nazis and Japs.

Except when he hid
in his bedroom on a three-day drunk,
he typed out complex itineraries, packed his trunk,

his matched luggage
and pocketed a confirmed reservation,
his heart already pushing over the red routes of the nation.

I sit at my desk
each night with no place to go,
opening the wrinkled maps of Milwaukee and Buffalo,

the whole U.S.,
its cemeteries, its arbitrary time zones,
through routes like small veins, capitals like small stones.

He died on the road,
his heart pushed from neck to back,
his white hanky signaling from the window of the Cadillac.

My husband,
as blue-eyed as a picture book, sells wool:
boxes of card waste, laps and rovings he can pull

to the thread
and say *Leicester, Rambouillet, Merino,*
a half-blood, it's greasy and thick, yellow as old snow.

And when you drive off, my darling,
Yes, sir! Yes, sir! It's one for my dame,
your sample cases branded with my father's name,

your itinerary open,
its tolls ticking and greedy,
its highways built up like new loves, raw and speedy.

January 25, 1962

Driving Nails

Gary L. Lark

I learned to walk stud walls
setting rafters when I was six.
I straightened nails for my father
to re-drive, piecing a home together
after work or on weekends.

We were called Okies by some
when we moved to the valley,
putting up our tar-papered shack.
Two years later a house was rising
to face them across the pasture.

The only plans were sketched
on a six inch pad, but all the corners
were true. The septic tank hole
was dug with pick and shovel.
Lumber carted home from the mill.

The only time help came
was when we poured the foundation.
Guys from the mill rode springing planks
to deliver tons of wet concrete by wheelbarrow,
tamped down with shovel handles.

My father beveled the molding,
drilled and set each piece of hardwood flooring,
not a nail would show. I crawled insulation

into tight places above the ceiling
and helped with rolled roofing.

Nobody mentioned our low rank
when my mother joined the garden club.
And she never mentioned the hurt
they had caused—just came home
and parked the Buick in the shack.

Men Throwing Bricks

Michael Chitwood

The one on the ground lofts two at a time
with just the right lift for them to finish
their rise as the one on the scaffold turns
to accept them like a gift and place them
on the growing stack. They chime slightly
on the catch. You'd have to do this daily,
morning and afternoon, not to marvel.

Traffic

Donald Hall

Trucks and station wagons, VWs, old Chevys, Pintos,
drive stop-and-go down Whitney Avenue this hot
May day, bluing the coarse air, past graveyard and florist,
past this empty brick building covered
with ivy like a Mayan temple,
like a pyramid grown over with jungle vines,

                                                 I walk around

the building as if I were dreaming it; as if
I had left my planet at twenty
and wandered a lifetime among galaxies and come home
to find my planet aged ten thousand years,
ruined, grown over,
the people gone, ruin taking their places.

                                              They

have gone into graveyards, who worked at this loading dock
wearing brown uniforms with the pink and blue lettering
of the Brock-Hall Dairy:
Freddie Bauer is dead, who watched over the stockroom;
Agnes McSparren is dead, who wrote figures in books
at a yellow wooden desk; Harry Bailey is dead,
who tested for bacteria
wearing a white coat; Karl Kapp is dead,
who loaded his van at dawn,
conveyor belt supplying butter, cottage cheese, heavy cream,
B. buttermilk, A with its creamline—
and left white bottles at backdoors in North Haven and Hamden

for thirty years; my father is dead
and my grandfather.
                    I stand by the fence at lot's end
where the long stable stood—
fifty workhorses alive
in the suburbs, chestnuts with thick manes, their hooves
the size of oak stumps, that pulled forty thousand quarts
through mists in the early morning to sleeping doorsteps,
until new trucks jammed the assembly lines
when the war ended.
                    I separate ivy
like long hair over a face
to gaze into the room where the bottlewasher
stretched its aluminum length like an Airstream trailer.
When our teacher brought the first grade to the dairy,
men in white caps stacked dirty bottles
at the machine's end, and we heard them clink
forty feet to where they rode out shining
on a belt to another machine
that turned them instantly white, as if someone said a word
that turned them white. I was proud
of my father and grandfather,
of my last name.
                    Here is the place
that was lettered with my father's name,
where he parked his Oldsmobile in the fifties.
I came to the plant with him one summer
when I was at college, and we walked across blacktop
where people my age washed trucks;
both of us smiled and looked downwards. That year
the business grossed sixteen million dollars
with four hundred people bottling and delivering milk

and Agnes McSparren was boss
over thirty women.
                        At the roof's edge,
imperial Roman cement urns
flourish and decorate exhausted air.
Now suburbs have migrated north
leaving Whitneyville behind, with its dead factory
beside a dead movie. They lived in Whitneyville
mostly—Freddie Bauer, Agnes McSparren, Karl Kapp,
Harry Bailey—who walked their lives
into brick, whose hours turned into milk,
who left their lives inside pitted brick
that disappears beneath ivy
for a thousand years, until the archeologist from a far galaxy
chops with his machete . . .
                        No, no, no.
In a week or a year
the wrecker's derrick with fifteen-ton cement ball
on a flatbed trailer
will stop traffic as it squeezes up Whitney Avenue,
and brick will collapse, and dump trucks take clean fill
for construction rising from a meadow
ten miles in the country.
                        I wait
for the traffic to pause, shift, and enter the traffic.

Small Pleasures
Mojave Desert, California

Greg Pape

Noon, one hundred fourteen degrees, no breeze
except the breeze we make
going ten miles an hour in the pickup,
no road, just open flat desert, low brush
and scattered rock, the Mojave
somewhere west of Edwards Air Force Base.
We're eating our sandwiches, the boss and I,
drinking cups of cold water from the thermos jug
on the seat between us. We carry
three gallons of water for each man
to get us through to four o'clock,
when we head for cold beer at the bar.
He hasn't said anything for some time,
just chews and drinks, chews and drinks,
stares out at the heat waves
as the pickup bumps along. Covered with dust
and oil, we've been out here since five a.m.
working on the road. Now we're leaving
the road behind. Last night, stopped
at a phone booth on the way to the motel,
I watched moths swarm at the light
while he tried to call home, was it?
Something was wrong, bad connection, something.
He got angry, yanked the phone off the cord
and threw it on the ground. He didn't try
to explain, and I didn't ask.
We went to our rooms and slept.

We've finished our lunch and cigarettes.
I look over thinking to say something
about how a day like this makes me appreciate
small pleasures, a little shade, this cushioned
seat, a cold tomato with salt, but his
fifty-year-old eyes are closed, his head
fallen to one side, mouth open, hands
in his lap, no longer steering.
Out here it doesn't seem to matter.
Even the snakes, tortoises, and horned lizards
are underground. It's a big desert
and we're all alone. I lean back,
close my eyes. This too
is a pleasure, moving off into the open
where the work is never done.

Feeding Time

Maxine Kumin

Sunset. I pull on
parka, boots, mittens, hat,
cross the road to the paddock.
Cat comes,
the skinny, feral tom
who took us on last fall.
Horses are waiting.
Each enters his box
in the order they've all
agreed on, behind my back.
Cat supervises from the molding cove.
Hay first. Water next. Grain last.
Check thermometer: seven degrees.
Check latches. Leave.

The sky
goes purple, blotched with red.
Feed dog next.
I recross the road to the woodshed.
Snappish moment with cat
but no real contest.
Wag, wag, kerchunk! The plate
is polished. Dog
grovels his desire
to go inside, lie like a log
by the fire.

Two above.
Above, it's gray
with meager afterglow.
Feed birds next.
I wade by way
of footprint wells through deep snow
to cylinders on trees.
Cat follows
observing distribution
of sunflower seeds.
Checks out each heel-toe
I've stepped in, in case
something he needs,
something small and foolish lurks.
No luck.

Penultimate,
cat gets
enormous supper:
chicken gizzards! Attacks
these like a cougar
tearing, but not in haste.
Retires to barn loft
to sleep in the hay,
or pretends to. Maybe
he catches dessert this way.

Now us,
Dear One. My soup, your bread
in old blue bowls that have withstood
thirty years of slicings and soppings.
Where are the children
who ate their way through helpings

of cereals and stews
to designs of horse, pig,
sheep on view
at the bottom of the dish?
Crying, *when I grow up*,
children have got their wish.

It's ten below.
The house dozes.
The attic stringers cough.
Time that blows on the kettle's rim
waits to carry us off.

Butchering the Crippled Heifer

Linda M. Hasselstrom

First:
    aim the pistol at her ear. Stand close.
    She chews slowly, eyes closed. Fire.
    She drops. Kicks. Sighs.
    Cut her throat and stand back.
    Blood bubbles and steams.

Then:
    wrap chain around each ankle,
    spread the back legs with a singletree.
    The tractor growls, lifting;
    the carcass sways.

Next:
    drive the knife point in,
    open the belly like tearing cloth,
    the blade just under the skin.
    Cut around the empty udder.
    Don't puncture the stomach.
    Sheathe the knife and reach in.
    Wrap your bare arms around the slick guts.
    Press your face against warm flesh.
    Find the ridge of backbone; tear the
    membranes loose. Hold the anus shut;
    pull hard until the great blue stomach bag
    spills into the tub at your feet.

Jerk the windpipe loose with a sucking moan,
her last sound.

Straighten:
    Breathe blood-scent, clean digested grass.
    Plunge one arm into the tub, cut loose the heart,
    and squeeze the last clots out; slice the liver
    away from the green gall, put it all in cool water
    Eat fresh liver and onions for supper,
    baked heart tomorrow.

Finally:
    Cut off the head and feet,
    haul them and the guts to the pasture:
    coyotes will feast tonight.

Then:
    pull the skin taut with one hand,
    slice the spider web of tissue with care.
    Save the tail for soup.
    Drape the hide on the fence.

Let her hang:
    sheet-wrapped, through three cool October days,
    while leaves yellow and
    coyotes howl thanksgiving.

Cut her up:
    bring one quarter at a time to the kitchen table.
    Toss bones into the big soup kettle
    to simmer, the marrow sliding out. Chunk
    scraps, pack them in canning jars.

Cut thick red steaks, wrap them in white paper,
labeled for the freezer.

Make meat:
    worship at a bloody altar, knives singing praises
    for the heifer's health, for flesh she made
    of hay pitched at forty below zero last winter.

Your hands are red with her blood,
slick with her fat.

You know
where your next meal is coming from.

Meat

August Kleinzahler

How much meat moves
Into the city each night
The decks of its bridges tremble
In the liquefaction of sodium light
And the moon a chemical orange

Semitrailers strain their axles
Shivering as they take the long curve
Over warehouses and lofts
The wilderness of streets below
The mesh of it
With Joe on the front stoop smoking
And Louise on the phone with her mother

Out of the haze of industrial meadows
They arrive, numberless
Hauling tons of dead lamb
Bone and flesh and offal
Miles to the ports and channels
Of the city's shimmering membrane
A giant breathing cell
Exhaling its waste
From the stacks by the river
And feeding through the night

The Bad Old Days

Kenneth Rexroth

The summer of nineteen eighteen
I read *The Jungle* and *The
Research Magnificent.* That fall
My father died and my aunt
Took me to Chicago to live.
The first thing I did was to take
A streetcar to the stockyards.
In the winter afternoon,
Gritty and fetid, I walked
Through the filthy snow, through the
Squalid streets, looking shyly
Into the people's faces,
Those who were home in the daytime.
Debauched and exhausted faces,
Starved and looted brains, faces
Like the faces in the senile
And insane wards of charity
Hospitals. Predatory
Faces of little children,
Then as the soiled twilight darkened,
Under the green gas lamps, and the
Sputtering purple arc lamps,
The faces of the men coming
Home from work, some still alive with
The last pulse of hope or courage,
Some sly and bitter, some smart and
Silly, most of them already

Broken and empty, no life,
Only blinding tiredness, worse
Than any tired animal.
The sour smells of a thousand
Suppers of fried potatoes and
Fried cabbage bled into the street.
I was giddy and sick, and out
Of my misery I felt rising
A terrible anger and out
Of the anger, an absolute vow.
Today the evil is clean
And prosperous, but it is
Everywhere, you don't have to
Take a streetcar to find it,
And it is the same evil.
And the misery, and the
Anger, and the vow are the same.

12

OUT WEST

A Home on the Range

Anonymous

Oh, give me a home where the buffalo roam,
Where the deer and the antelope play,
Where seldom is heard a discouraging word
And the skies are not cloudy all day.

There's a land in the West where nature is blessed
With a beauty so vast and austere,
And though you have flown off to cities unknown,
Your memories bring you back here.

Where the air is so pure, the zephyrs so free,
The breezes so balmy and light,
I would not exchange my home on the range
For all of the cities so bright.

The canyons and buttes like old twisted roots
And the sandstone of ancient stream beds
In the sunset they rise to dazzle our eyes
With their lavenders, yellows, and reds.

How often at night when the heavens are bright
With the light of the glittering stars,
Have I stood here amazed and asked as I gazed
If their glory exceeds that of ours.

I love the wild flowers in this dear land of ours,
The curlew I love to hear scream,

And I love the white rocks and the antelope flocks
That graze on the mountain-tops green.

Oh, give me a land where the bright diamond sand
Flows leisurely down to the stream;
Where the graceful white swan goes gliding along
Like a maid in a heavenly dream.

The red man was pressed from this part of the West
And is likely no more to return
To the banks of Red River where seldom if ever
Their flickering campfires burn.

Home, home on the range,
Where the deer and the antelope play,
Where seldom is heard a discouraging word
And the skies are not cloudy all day.

When it comes my time to leave you behind
And sail off to regions unknown,
Please lay my remains out on the plains,
Lay me down in my prairie home.

Accountability

William Stafford

Cold nights outside the taverns in Wyoming
pickups and big semis lounge idling, letting their
haunches twitch now and then in gusts of powder snow,
their owners inside for hours, forgetting as well
as they can the miles, the circling plains, the still town
that connects to nothing but cold and space and a few
stray ribbons of pavement, icy guides to nothing
but bigger towns and other taverns that glitter and wait:
Denver, Cheyenne.

Hibernating in the library of the school on the hill
a few pieces by Thomas Aquinas or Saint Teresa
and the fragmentary explorations of people like Alfred
North Whitehead crouch and wait amid research folders
on energy and military recruitment posters glimpsed
by the hard stars. The school bus by the door, a yellow
mound, clangs open and shut as the wind finds a loose
door and worries it all night, letting the hollow
students count off and break up and blow away
over the frozen ground.

Alien

Jim Harrison

It was one of those mornings when my feet seemed unaware of each other and I walked slowly up a canyon wash to avoid tripping. It was warmish at dawn but the sun wouldn't quite come out, having missed a number of good chances, or so I thought studying the antic clouds that were behaving as sloppily as the government. I was looking for a wildflower, the penstemon, but stopped at a rock pool in a miniature marsh seeing a Mojave rattlesnake curled up in the cup of a low-slung boulder. Since this snake can kill a cow or horse I detoured through a dense thicket then glimpsed the small opening of a side canyon I had not noticed in my seventeen years of living down the road. How could I have missed it except that it's my habit to miss a great deal? And then the sun came out and frightened me as if I had stumbled onto a well-hidden house of the gods, roofless and only a hundred feet long, backed by a sheer wall of stone. I smelled the telltale urine of a mountain lion but no cave was visible until I looked up at a passing Mexican jay who shrieked the usual warning. We move from fear to fear. I knew the lion would be hiding there in the daytime more surely than I had seen the snake. They weren't guardians. This is where they lived. These small rock cathedrals are spread around the landscape in hundreds of variations but this one had the rawness of the unseen, giving me an edge of discomfort rarely felt in nature except in Ecuador and the Yucatán where I had appeared as a permanent stranger. I sat down with my back tight against a sheer wall thinking that the small cave entrance I faced by craning my neck must be the home of the old female lion seen around here not infrequently and that she could only enter from a crevasse at the top, downward into her cave. This is nature without us. This is someone's home where I don't belong.

A Walk

Gary Snyder

Sunday the only day we don't work:
Mules farting around the meadow,
                        Murphy fishing,
The tent flaps in the warm
Early sun: I've eaten breakfast and I'll
                take a walk
To Benson Lake. Packed a lunch,
Goodbye. Hopping on creekbed boulders
Up the rock throat three miles
                Piute Creek—
In steep gorge glacier-slick rattlesnake country
Jump, land by a pool, trout skitter,
The clear sky. Deer tracks.
Bad place by a falls, boulders big as houses,
Lunch tied to belt,
I stemmed up a crack and almost fell
But rolled out safe on a ledge
                and ambled on.
Quail chicks freeze underfoot, color of stone
Then run cheep! away, hen quail fussing.
Craggy west end of Benson Lake—after edging
Past dark creek pools on a long white slope—
Lookt down in the ice-black lake
                lined with cliff
From far above: deep shimmering trout.
A lone duck in a gunsightpass
                steep side hill

Through slide-aspen and talus, to the east end,
Down to grass, wading a wide smooth stream
Into camp. At last.
                    By the rusty three-year-
Ago left-behind cookstove
Of the old trail crew,
Stoppt and swam and ate my lunch.

Missoula in a Dusty Light

John Haines

Walking home through the tall
Montana twilight,
leaves were moving in the gutters
and a little dust . . .

I saw beyond the roofs and chimneys
a cloud like a hill of smoke,
amber and a dirty grey. And a wind
began from the street corners
and rutted alleys,
out of year-end gardens, weed lots
and trash bins;
           the yellow air
came full of specks and ash,
noiseless, crippled things that crashed
and flew again . . .
grit and the smell of rain.
And then a steady sound,
as if an army or a council,
long-skirted, sweeping the stone,
were gathering near;
disinherited and vengeful people,
scuffing their bootheels,
rolling tin cans before them.

And quieter still behind them
the voices of birds

and whispering brooms:
                "This land
has bitter roots, and seeds
that crack and spill in the wind . . ."

I halted under a blowing light
to listen, to see;
and it was the bleak Montana wind
sweeping the leaves and dust
along the street.

Bronco Busting, Event #1

May Swenson

The stall so tight he can't raise heels or knees
when the cowboy, coccyx to bareback, touches down

tender as a deerfly, forks him, gripping the rope-
handle over the withers, testing the cinch,

as if hired to lift a cumbersome piece of brown
luggage, while assistants perched on the rails arrange

the kicker, a foam-rubber band around the narrowest,
most ticklish part of the loins, leaning full weight

on neck and rump to keep him throttled, this horse,
"Firecracker," jacked out of the box through the sprung

gate, in the same second raked both sides of the belly
by ratchets on booted heels, bursts into five-way

motion: bucks, pitches, swivels, humps, and twists,
an all-over-body-sneeze that must repeat

until the flapping bony lump attached to his spine is gone.
A horn squawks. Up from the dust gets a buster named Tucson.

The Saturday Matinee

Jon Bowerman

I still recall that early day
When we went to the Saturday matinee
There was Roy and Hoppy and Lash LaRue
Gene Autry and a lot of others too.
They rode good horses and they all packed guns
But it seems they never killed anyone.
They never ran from a stand up fight
But they always fought fair and did what was right.
When threatened by a rustler band
They shot the guns from the outlaws' hands.
They had truth and honor and all the traits
That makes a hero really great.
And after the Saturday matinee
When we all went outside to play
We lived by the "The Code" and could understand
Only shoot at the guns in the bad guys' hands
Back when playin' cowboys was all in fun
And real heroes never killed anyone.

Morning News in the Bighorn Mountains

William Notter

The latest movie star is drunk in spite of rehab,
two or three cities had extraordinary killings,
and expensive homes are sliding off the hills
or burning again. There's an energy crisis on,
and peace in the Middle East is close as ever.
In Wyoming, just below timberline,
meteors and lightning storms
keep us entertained at night. Last week,
a squirrel wrecked the mountain bluebirds' nest.
I swat handfuls of moths in the cabin
and set them out each day,
but the birds will not come back to feed.
It snowed last in June, four inches
the day before the solstice. But summer
is winding down—the grass was frosted
this morning when we left the ranger station.
Yellow-bellied marmots are burrowing
under the outhouse vault, and ravens have left the ridges
to gorge on Mormon crickets in the meadows.
Flakes of obsidian and red flint
knapped from arrowheads hundreds of years ago
appear in the trails each day,
and the big fish fossil in the limestone cliff
dissolves a little more with every rain.

Boulder Dam

May Sarton

Not in the cities, not among fabricated towers,
Not on the superhighways has the land been matched.
Beside the mountains, man's invention cowers.
And in a country various and wild and beautiful
How cheap the new car and the lighted movie look.
We have been hourly aware of a failure to live,
Monotonous poverty of spirit and the lack of love.

But here among hills bare and desert-red,
A violent precipice, a dizzy white curve falls
Hundreds of feet through rock to the deep canyon-bed;
A beauty sheer and clean and without error,
It stands with the created sapphire lake behind it,
It stands, a work of man as noble as the hills,
And it is faith as well as water that it spills.

Not built on terror like the empty pyramid,
Not built to conquer but to illuminate a world:
It is the human answer to a human need,
Power in absolute control, freed as a gift,
A pure creative act, God when the world was born!
It proves that we have built for life and built for love
And when we all are dead, this dam will stand and give.

Two Girls

Jim Harrison

Late November (full moon last night),
a cold Patagonia moon, the misty air
tinkled slightly, a rank-smelling bull
in the creek bottom seemed to be crying.
Coyotes yelped up the canyon
where they took a trip-wire photo of a jaguar
last spring. I hope he's sleeping or eating
a delicious deer. Our two little girl dogs
are peeing in the midnight yard, nervous
about the bull. They can't imagine a jaguar.

The Trestle

Raymond Carver

I've wasted my time this morning, and I'm deeply ashamed.
I went to bed last night thinking about my dad.
About that little river we used to fish—Butte Creek—
near Lake Almanor. Water lulled me to sleep.
In my dream, it was all I could do not to get up
and move around. But when I woke early this morning
I went to the telephone instead. Even though
the river was flowing down there in the valley,
in the meadows, moving through ditch clover.
Fir trees stood on both sides of the meadows. And I was there.
A kid sitting on a timber trestle, looking down.
Watching my dad drink from his cupped hands.
Then he said, "This water's so good.
I wish I could give my mother some of this water."
My dad still loved her, though she was dead
and he'd been away from her for a long time.
He had to wait some more years
until he could go where she was. But he loved
this country where he found himself. The West.
For thirty years it had him around the heart,
and then it let him go. He went to sleep one night
in a town in northern California
and didn't wake up. What could be simpler?

I wish my own life, and death, could be so simple.
So that when I woke on a fine morning like this,
after being somewhere I wanted to be all night,

somewhere important, I could move most naturally
and without thinking about it, to my desk.

Say I did that, in the simple way I've described.
From bed to desk back to childhood.
From there it's not so far to the trestle.
And from the trestle I could look down
and see my dad when I needed to see him.
My dad drinking that cold water. My sweet father.
The river, its meadows, and firs, and the trestle.
That. Where I once stood.

I wish I could do that
without having to plead with myself for it.
And feel sick of myself
for getting involved in lesser things.
I know it's time I changed my life.
This life—the one with its complications
and phone calls—is unbecoming,
and a waste of time.
I want to plunge my hands in clear water. The way
he did. Again and then again.

13

SHOW BUSINESS

Piano Dreams

Marcia F. Brown

Sometimes I'm Bobby Short
at the Carlyle Hotel where fur-tipped
women trip in from the cold
on the thick padded arms of their men.
They sparkle with new snow
and old money. But it's me
they want to see. Leaning
into the keys, I play *Autumn in New York*,
Misty and *I've Got You Under My Skin*.
The golden women tilt their heads
with a faraway look in their eyes,
and run jeweled fingers tenderly
over crystal champagne rims.
I launch into *You Do Something to Me*
and they raise their glasses
and drink.

Sometimes I'm back
in that huge green ballroom
with the white doors
over the restaurant on High Street.
It's late spring—recital time—
and I'm supposed to practice my solo
here for 45 minutes. It's hot
so I'm thinking about the community pool, not
the *Mazurka* from *Les Sylphides*, and how
I'll ask my mother to drop me off there

after lunch. But then Stephanie Woodruff
from homeroom steps in the white door.
"Oh that's so pretty," she says, "Don't stop playing."
And she executes a little faux mazurka step
around the room, laughing—
and I laugh too and play it faster
and better than I ever have.
And she keeps dancing and I keep playing
and this is how I learn
whatever it is I know about art
and everything I know
about imagination.
And sometimes
I'm my Dad's old friend, Morty Ackerman
from Albany, who finally got tired
of hauling his combo from one
snowed-in lounge to another,
and took a job at a nudist colony
outside Sarasota. He said clothing
was optional for the staff and the talent.
He usually wore Bermuda shorts and a bow tie.
But on New Year's Eve, the story went,
just his "white tie and tail."
He claimed the ladies didn't wait
to be asked onto the dance floor—they just drifted
up there by themselves, dipping and twirling
like nymphs around the Steinway. He said
he played like some kind of crazed piano god.
He said they danced
right into January.

Late Wonders

W.S. Merwin

In Los Angeles the cars are flowing
through the white air
and the news of bombings

at Universal Studios
you can ride through an avalanche
if you have never
ridden through an avalanche

with your ticket
you can ride on a trolley
before which the Red
Sea parts
just the way it did
for Moses

you can see Los Angeles
destroyed hourly
you can watch the avenue named for somewhere else
the one on which you know you are
crumple and vanish incandescent
with a terrible cry
all around you
rising from the houses and families

of everyone you have seen all day
driving shopping talking eating

it's only a movie
it's only a beam of light

In Chandler Country

Dana Gioia

California night. The Devil's wind,
the Santa Ana, blows in from the east,
raging through the canyon like a drunk
screaming in a bar.
                  The air tastes like
a stubbed-out cigarette. But why complain?
The weather's fine as long as you don't breathe.
Just lean back on the sweat-stained furniture,
lights turned out, windows shut against the storm,
and count your blessings.
                  Another sleepless night,
when every wrinkle in the bedsheet scratches
like a dry razor on a sunburned cheek,
when even ten-year whiskey tastes like sand,
and quiet women in the kitchen run
their fingers on the edges of a knife
and eye their husbands' necks. I wish them luck.

Tonight it seems that if I took the coins
out of my pocket and tossed them in the air
they'd stay a moment glistening like a net
slowly falling through dark water.
                  I remember
the headlights of the cars parked on the beach,
the narrow beams dissolving on the dark
surface of the lake, voices arguing
about the forms, the crackling radio,

the sheeted body lying on the sand,
the trawling net still damp beside it. No,
she wasn't beautiful—but at that age
when youth itself becomes a kind of beauty—
"Taking good care of your clients, Marlowe?"

Relentlessly the wind blows on. Next door
catching a scent, the dogs begin to howl.
Lean, furious, raw-eyed from the storm,
packs of coyotes come down from the hills
where there is nothing left to hunt.

Nancy Drew

Ron Koertge

Merely pretty, she made up for it with vim.
And she got to say things like, "But, gosh,
what if these plans should fall into the wrong
hands?" And it was pretty clear she didn't mean
plans for a party or a trip to the museum, but
something involving espionage and a Nazi or two.

In fact, the handsome exchange student turns
out to be a Fascist sympathizer. When he snatches
Nancy along with some blueprints, she knows he
has something more sinister in mind than kissing
with his mouth open.

Locked in the pantry of an abandoned farm house,
Nancy makes a radio out of a shoelace and a muffin.
Pretty soon the police show up, and everything's
hunky dory.

Nancy accepts their thanks, but she's subdued.
It's not like her to fall for a cad. Even as she plans
a short vacation to sort out her emotions she knows
there will be a suspicious waiter, a woman in a green
off the shoulder dress, and her very jittery husband.

Very well. But no more handsome boys like the last one:
the part in his hair that was sheer propulsion, that way
he had of lifting his eyes to hers over the custard,
those feelings that made her not want to be brave
confident and daring, polite, sensitive and caring.

Studs Terkel

Gary Johnson

A radio man from the Great Depression
With his wild white hair and wavy eyes,
Talking to cranky skeptics and old sweetie-pies.
Talking to strangers was his sacred profession,
He was born on the day the Titanic went down,
Lived in Chicago on the North Side.
At 96 he made his exit on a string of old jokes,
Lit a smoke, poured a drink, and died,
Raising one hand to make a blessing on the town,
Took a last swallow, and waved to the folks,
    Saying, "So long it's been good to know you,
    And I've got to be drifting along."

Live at the Village Vanguard

Sebastian Matthews

Near the end of Bill Evans' "Porgy (I Loves You, Porgy)"
played live at the Village Vanguard and added as an extra track
on *Waltz for Debby* (a session made famous by the death
of the trio's young bassist in a car crash) a woman laughs.
There's been background babble bubbling up the whole set.
You get used to the voices percolating at the songs' fringes,
the clink of glasses and tips of silver on hard plates. Listen
to the recording enough and you almost accept the aural clutter
as another percussive trick the drummer pulls out, like brushes
on a snare. But this woman's voice stands out for its carefree
audacity, how it broadcasts the lovely ascending stair of her happiness.
Evans has just made one of his elegant, casual flights up an octave
and rests on its landing, notes spilling from his left hand
like sunlight, before coming back down into the tune's lush
living-room of a conclusion. The laugh begins softly, subsides,
then lifts up to step over the bass line: five short bursts of pleasure
pushed out of what can only be a long lovely tan throat. Maybe
Evans smiles to himself when he hears it, leaving a little space
between the notes he's cobbled to close the song; maybe
the man she's with leans in, first to still her from the laugh
he's just coaxed from her, then to caress the cascade of her hair
that hangs, lace curtain, in the last vestiges of spotlight stippling the table.

Minor Seventh

Jeffrey Bean

Foghorns, grackles, wheat fields sighing in wind. The night hawk's ricochet. *You better come on in my kitchen.* Mixolydian trumpet runs boiling up the Mississippi, turning into urban blues and smokestacks over Gary, Indiana. Hymns. Grief. The hiss of sprinklers in timber yards, brawl of log trucks crawling up Mt. Hood. Chainsaws, see-saws, sneakers squeaking in high school gyms. *Have you driven a ford lately?* Field hollers. Sorrow. Fat fathers riding their mowers' thick chords. Throngs of Santa Clauses all across Wisconsin ringing bells in snow in front of Wal-Marts. Musac at Costco, Osco, Piggly Wiggly, Winn-Dixie. Arawaks' shouting, the Santa Maria creaking onto shore. Cell phones, car alarms, laptops, the air raid siren's range. *Achy Breaky Heart* in the flamingo light of roller rinks. The wheeze of progress. The forests of Mississippi echoing with *Me and the devil was walking side by side.* Grind of church organs, cotton gins, sledge hammers knocking into granite. No one listening to Monk play *Crepuscule with Nellie* at The Open Door. Toyotas starting, crows screaming, a rabbit snatched by an owl. *Gimme a pigsfoot and a bottle of beer.* Reverend Dimmesdale speaking in tongues of flame. Michael Buffer crooning *Let's get ready to rumble!* Chants at NBA games. Weeping. *St Louis woman, where's your diamond ring?*

Kryptonite

Ron Koertge

Lois liked to see the bullets bounce
off Superman's chest, and of course
she was proud when he leaned into
a locomotive and saved the crippled
orphan who had fallen on the tracks.

Yet on those long nights when he was
readjusting longitude or destroying
a meteor headed right for some nun,
Lois considered carrying just a smidgen
of kryptonite in her purse or at least
making a tincture to dab behind her ears.

She pictured his knees giving way,
the color draining from his cheeks.
He'd lie on the couch like a guy with
the flu, too weak to paint the front
porch or take out the garbage. She
could peek down his tights or draw
on his cheek with a ball point. She
might even muss his hair and slap
him around.

"Hey, what'd I do?" he'd croak just
like a regular boyfriend. At last.

My Father Laughing in
the Chicago Theater

David Wagoner

His heavy body would double itself forward
At the waist, swell, and come heaving around
To slam at his seatback, making the screws groan
And squawk down half the row as it went tilting
Under my mother and me, under whoever
Was out of luck on the other side of him.
Like a boxer slipping punches, he'd lift his elbows
To flail and jerk, and his wide-open mouth
Would boom out four deep *haaa*'s to the end of his breath.

He was laughing at Burns and Allen or Jack Benny
In person or at his limitless engagement
With Groucho, Chico, and Harpo. While my mother
Sat there between us, gazing at the stage
And chuckling placidly, I watched with amazement
The spectacle of a helpless father, unmanned,
Disarmed by laughter. The tears would dribble
From under his bifocals, as real as sweat.
He would gape and gag, go limp, and spring back to life.

I would laugh too, but partly at him, afraid
Of becoming him. He could scowl anywhere,
Be solemn or blank in church or going to work,
Turn grim with a cold chisel, or he could smile
At babies or football games, but he only laughed

There in that theater. And up the aisle
And through the lobby to the parking lot
And all the way home, I'd see the glow on his cheeks
Fade to the usual hectic steelmill sunburn.

By bedtime he was as somber as himself:
Two hundred and twenty horizontal pounds
Of defensive lineman, of open-hearth melter
Who could take the temperature of molten steel
At a glance, who never swore or told a joke.
Once, Jimmy Durante stopped, glared down at him,
And slapped his sides, getting an extra laugh
From my father's laugh, then stiff-leg-strutted away,
Tipping his old hat in gratitude.

Ballet Blanc

Katha Pollitt

Baryshnikov leaps higher than your heart
in the moonlit forest, center stage, and pleads
with the ghostly corps, who pirouette, gauzed white
and powdered blue, like pearls, the star Sylphides

of Paris, 1841. You swoon
back in red plush. Oboes, adagio,
sing *love is death*—but death's this lustrous queen
who twirls forever on one famous toe

while hushed in shadows, tier on golden tier
swirls to apotheosis in the ceiling.
Miles away, through clouds, one chandelier
swings dizzily. What feeling

sweeps you? Dinner's roses and tall candles,
a certain wine-flushed face, your new blue dress
merge with the scented crush of silks and sables—
through which, you're more and more aware, two eyes

stroke, meltingly, your neck. You glow, you sway,
it's as though the audience were dancing too
and with a last, stupendous tour jeté
turned for a solo suddenly to *you*

and you become the Duke, the Queen, Giselle,
and waltz in a whirl of white through the painted grove,

your gestures as extravagant as tulle,
as wild as nineteenth-century hopeless love,

as grand as bravo! and brava! On wings,
you splurge and take a taxi home instead.
The park looms rich and magical. It's spring,
almost. You float upstairs and into bed

and into dreams so deep you never hear
how all night long that witch, your evil fairy,
crows her knowing cackle in your ear:
Tomorrow you will wake up ordinary.

The Skokie Theatre

Edward Hirsch

Twelve years old and lovesick, bumbling
and terrified for the first time in my life,
but strangely hopeful, too, and stunned,
definitely stunned—I wanted to cry,
I almost started to sob when Chris Klein
actually touched me—oh God—below the belt
in the back row of the Skokie Theatre.
Our knees bumped helplessly, our mouths
were glued together like flypaper, our lips
were grinding in a hysterical grimace
while the most handsome man in the world
twitched his hips on the flickering screen
and the girls began to scream in the dark.
I didn't know one thing about the body yet,
about the deep foam filling my bones,
but I wanted to cry out in desolation
when she touched me again, when the lights
flooded on in the crowded theatre
and the other kids started to file
into the narrow aisles, into a lobby
of faded purple splendor, into the last
Saturday in August before she moved away.
I never wanted to move again, but suddenly
we were being lifted toward the sidewalk

in a crush of bodies, blinking, shy,
unprepared for the ringing familiar voices
and the harsh glare of sunlight, the brightness
of an afternoon that left us gripping
each other's hands, trembling and changed.

The Junior High School Band Concert

David Wagoner

When our semi-conductor
Raised his baton, we sat there
Gaping at *Marche Militaire*,
Our mouth-opening number.
It seemed faintly familiar
(We'd rehearsed it all that winter),
But we attacked in such a blur,
No army anywhere
On its stomach or all fours
Could have squeezed through our cross fire.

I played cornet, seventh chair
Out of seven, my embouchure
A glorified Bronx cheer
Through that three-keyed keyhole stopper
And neighborhood window slammer
Where mildew fought for air
At every exhausted corner,
My fingering still unsure
After scaling it for a year
Except on the spit-valve lever.

Each straight-faced mother and father
Retested his moral fiber
Against our traps and slurs
And the inadvertent whickers
Paradiddled by our snares,

And when the brass bulled forth
A blare fit to horn over
Jericho two bars sooner
Than Joshua's harsh measures,
They still had the nerve to stare.

By the last lost chord, our director
Looked older and soberer.
No doubt, in his mind's ear
Some band somewhere
In some Music of some Sphere
Was striking a note as pure
As the wishes of Franz Schubert,
But meanwhile here we were:
A lesson in everything minor,
Decomposing our first composer.

Dance Suite: Hip Hop

W.D. Snodgrass

Lined up
Girls and boys,
Coins in the drop slot; wind-up toys;
Necks that switch
Every which way;
Join the Hip Hop, rapping like a robot.

Streets full of busfumes; stairs full of shovin';
TV's full of promises: luxuries and lovin';
Oil's on the water; spray's on the pumpkin;
Aspirin's full of strychnine, cyanide or somethin'.

Wig-wag
Knee joints,
Elbows crimped to zig-zag points;
Wrists and ankles
Twisted into angles;
Splayed-out fingers clamping into fists.

Sidewalks full of garbage; pictures in the news;
Mayor's on the radio spouting out excuses;
Bars on the storefronts; landlord's on the way;
Cops have got their Spring list—they'll make it pay.

Nuts and bolts
Charged by volts
Jumpstart into spastic jerks and jolts;

Gears and notches
Grinding crotches,
Juicing up the parts of the fools that watch us.

Ground's full of chemicals; ocean's full of waste;
Brother's full of steroids; meat got no taste;
Ceilings full of roaches; rats around the cradle;
Everybody's learned to read the lies on the label.

Swirl around
Clown, on the ground,
Twirling like a dervish whirls, upside down;
Legs there,
Kicking in the air,
Striking like scorpions or Medusa hair.

A bullet's in the chamber; needle's in the vein;
Leg's set in plaster; no time for pain;
Street's full of dealers; girls are on the curbs;
Make a killing fast and get out for the suburbs.

Shift your shoulder
Like a soldier
Ant, an identical mannekin or clone;
Who can hurt a tall doll
Rigid and mechanical
Dancing the dictates of a microphone?

Movie-Going

John Hollander

Drive-ins are out, to start with. One must always be
Able to see the over-painted Moorish ceiling
Whose pinchbeck jazz gleams even in the darkness, calling
The straying eye to feast on it, and glut, then fall
Back to the sterling screen again. One needs to feel
That the two empty, huddled, dark stage-boxes keep
Empty for kings. And having frequently to cope
With the abominable goodies, overflow
Bulk and (finally) exploring hands of flushed
Close neighbors gazing beadily out across glum
Distances is, after all, to keep the gleam
Alive of something rather serious, to keep
Faith, perhaps, with the City. When as children our cup
Of joys ran over the special section, and we clutched
Our ticket stubs and followed the bouncing ball, no clash
Of cymbals at the start of the stage-show could abash
Our third untiring time around. When we came back,
Older, to cop an endless series of feels, we sat
Unashamed beneath the bare art-nouveau bodies, set
High on the golden, after-glowing proscenium when
The break had come. And still, now as always, once
The show is over and we creep into the dull
Blaze of mid-afternoon sunshine, the hollow dole
Of the real descends on everything and we can know
That we have been in some place wholly elsewhere, a night
At noonday, not without dreams, whose portals shine

(Not ivory, not horn in ever-changing shapes)
But made of some weird, clear substance not often used for gates.

Stay for the second feature on a double bill
Always: it will teach you how to love, how not to live,
And how to leave the theater for that unlit, aloof
And empty world again. 'B'-pictures showed us: shooting
More real than singing or making love; the shifting
Ashtray upon the mantel, moved by some idiot
Between takes, helping us learn beyond a trace of doubt
How fragile are imagined scenes; the dimming-out
Of all the brightness of the clear and highly lit
Interior of the hero's cockpit, when the stock shot
Of ancient dive-bombers peeling off cuts in, reshapes
Our sense of what is, finally, plausible; the grays
Of living rooms, the blacks of cars whose window glass
At night allows the strips of fake Times Square to pass
Jerkily by on the last ride; even the patch
Of sudden white, and inverted letters dashing
Up during the projectionist's daydream, dying
Quickly—these are the colors of our inner life.

Never ignore the stars, of course. But above all,
Follow the asteroids as well: though dark, they're more
Intense for never glittering; anyone can admire
Sparklings against a night sky, but against a bright
Background of prominence, to feel the Presences burnt
Into no fiery fame should be a more common virtue.
For, just as Vesta has no atmosphere, no verdure
Burgeons on barren Ceres, bit-players never surge
Into the rhythms of expansion and collapse, such
As all the flaming bodies live and move among.
But there, more steadfast than stars are, loved for their being,
Not for their burning, move the great Characters: see

Thin Donald Meek, that shuffling essence ever so
Affronting to Eros and to Pride; the pair of bloated
Capitalists, Walter Connolly and Eugene Pallette, seated
High in their offices above New York; the evil,
Blackening eyes of Sheldon Leonard, and the awful
Stare of Eduardo Cianelli. Remember those who have gone—
(Where's bat-squeaking Butterfly McQueen? Will we see again
That ever-anonymous drunk, waxed-moustached, rubber-legged
Caught in revolving doors?) and think of the light-years logged
Up in those humbly noble orbits, where no hot
Spotlight of solar grace consumes some blazing hearts,
Bestowing the flimsy immortality of stars
For some great distant instant. Out of the darkness stares
Venus, who seems to be what once we were, the fair
Form of emerging love, her nitrous atmosphere
Hiding her prizes. Into the black expanse peers
Mars, whom we in time will come to resemble: parched,
Xanthine desolations, dead Cimmerian seas, the far
Distant past preserved in the blood-colored crusts; fire
And water both remembered only. Having shined
Means having died. But having been merely real, and shunned
Stardom, the planetoids are what we now are, humming
With us, above us, ever into the future, seeming
Ever to take the shapes of the world we wake to from dreams.

Always go in the morning if you can; it will
Be something more than habit if you do. Keep well
Away from most French farces. Try to see a set
Of old blue movies every so often, that the sight
Of animal doings out of the clothes of 'thirty-five
May remind you that even the natural act is phrased
In the terms and shapes of particular times and places.
Finally, remember always to honor the martyred dead.
The forces of darkness spread everywhere now, and the best

And brightest screens fade out, while many-antennaed beasts
Perch on the housetops, and along the grandest streets
Palaces crumble, one by one. The dimming starts
Slowly at first; the signs are few, as 'Movies are
Better than Ever,' 'Get More out of Life. See a Movie' Or
Else there's no warning at all and, Whoosh! the theater falls,
Alas, transmogrified: no double-feature fills
A gleaming marquee with promises, now only lit
With 'Pike and Whitefish Fresh Today' 'Drano' and 'Light
Or Dark Brown Sugar, Special.' Try never to patronize
Such places (or pass them by one day a year). The noise
Of movie mansions changing form, caught in the toils
Of our lives' withering, rumbles, resounds and tolls
The knell of neighborhoods. Do not forget the old
Places, for everyone's home has been a battlefield.

I remember: the RKO COLONIAL; the cheap
ARDEN and ALDEN both; LOEW'S LINCOLN SQUARE's bright shape;
The NEWSREEL; the mandarin BEACON, resplendently arrayed;
The tiny SEVENTY-SEVENTH STREET, whose demise I rued
So long ago; the eighty-first street, sunrise-hued,
RKO; and then LOEW'S at eighty-third, which had
The colder pinks of sunset on it; and then, back
Across Broadway again, and up, you disembarked
At the YORKTOWN and then the STODDARD, with their dark
Marquees; the SYMPHONY had a decorative disk
With elongated 'twenties nudes whirling in it;
(Around the corner the THALIA, daughter of memory! owed
Her life to Foreign Hits, in days when you piled your coat
High on your lap and sat, sweating and cramped, to catch
'La Kermesse Heroïque' every third week, and watched
Fritz Lang from among an audience of refugees, bewitched
By the sense of Crisis on and off that tiny bit
Of screen) Then north again: the RIVERSIDE, the bright

RIVIERA rubbing elbows with it; and right
Smack on a hundredth street, the MIDTOWN; and the rest
Of them: the CARLTON, EDISON, LOEW'S OLYMPIA, and best
Because, of course, the last of all, its final burst
Anonymous, the NEMO! These were once the pearls
Of two-and-a-half miles of Broadway! How many have paled
Into a supermarket's failure of the imagination?

Honor them all. Remember how once their splendor blazed
In sparkling necklaces across America's blasted
Distances and deserts: think how, at night, the fastest
Train might stop for water somewhere, waiting, faced
Westward, in deepening dusk, till ruby illuminations
Of something different from Everything Here, Now, shine
Out from the local Bijou, truest gem, the most bright
Because the most believed in, staving off the night
Perhaps, for a while longer with its flickering light.

These fade. All fade, Let us honor them with our own fading sight.

14

OCEAN BRINE

This Night Only

Kenneth Rexroth

[*Eric Satie: GYMNOPÉDIE # 1*]

Moonlight   now   on Malibu
The winter night   the few stars
Far away   millions   of miles
The sea   going on   and on
Forever   around   the earth
Far   and   far   as your lips   are near
Filled   with the same light   as your eyes
Darling   darling   darling
The future   is long gone by
And the past   will never happen
We have   only this
Our one forever
So small   so infinite
So brief   so vast
Immortal   as our hands that touch
Deathless   as the firelit wine we drink
Almighty   as this single kiss
That has no beginning
That will never
Never
End

Cape Cod

George Santayana

The low sandy beach and the thin scrub pine,
The wide reach of bay and the long sky line,—
    O, I am far from home!

The salt, salt smell of the thick sea air,
And the smooth round stones that the ebbtides wear,
    When will the good ship come?

The wretched stumps all charred and burned,
And the deep soft rut where the cartwheel turned,
    Why is the world so old?

The lapping wave, and the broad gray sky
Where the cawing crows and the slow gulls fly,—
    Where are the dead untold?

The thin, slant willows by the flooded bog,
The huge stranded hulk and the floating log,—
    Sorrow with life began!

And among the dark pines, and along the flat shore,
O the wind, and the wind, for evermore!
    What will become of man?

San Francisco Remembered

Philip Schultz

In summer the polleny light bounces off the white buildings
& you can see their spines & nerves & where the joints knot.
You've never seen such polleny light. The whole city shining
& the women wearing dresses so thin you see their wing-tipped hips
& their tall silvery legs alone can knock your eye out.
But this isn't about women. It's about the city of blue waters
& fog so thick it wraps round your legs & leaves glistening trails
along the dark winding streets. Once I followed such a trail
& wound up beside this redheaded woman who looked up & smiled
& let me tell you you don't see smiles like that in Jersey City.
She was wearing a black raincoat with two hundred pockets
& I wanted to put my hands in each one. But forget about her.
I was talking about the fog which steps up & taps your shoulder
like a panhandler who wants bus fare to a joint called The Paradise
& where else could this happen? On Sundays Golden Gate Park
is filled with young girls strolling the transplanted palms
& imported rhododendron beds. You should see the sunset
in their eyes & the sway, the proud sway of their young shoulders.
Believe me, it takes a day or two to recover. Or the trolleys clanking
down the steep hills—why you see legs flashing like mirrors!
Please, Lord, please let me talk about San Francisco. How
that gorilla of a bridge twists in the ocean wind & the earth
turns under your feet & at any moment the whole works can crack
& slip back into the sea like a giant being kicked off his raft
& now, if it's all right, I would like to talk about women . . .

The Place for No Story

Robinson Jeffers

The coast hills at Sovranes Creek;
No trees, but dark scant pasture drawn thin
Over rock shaped like flame;
The old ocean at the land's foot, the vast
Gray extension beyond the long white violence;
A herd of cows and the bull
Far distant, hardly apparent up the dark slope;
And the gray air haunted with hawks:
This place is the noblest thing I have ever seen. No
    imaginable
Human presence here could do anything
But dilute the lonely self-watchful passion.

The Large Starfish

Robert Bly

It is low tide. Fog. I have climbed down the cliffs from Pierce Ranch to the tide pools. Now the ecstasy of the low tide, kneeling down, alone. In six inches of clear water I notice a purple starfish—with nineteen arms! It is a delicate purple, the color of old carbon paper, or an attic dress . . . at the webs between fingers sometimes a more intense sunset red glows through. The fingers are relaxed . . . some curled up at the tips . . . with delicate rods . . . apparently globes . . . on top of each, as at World's Fairs, waving about. The starfish slowly moves up the groin of the rock . . . then back down . . . many of its arms rolled up now, lazily, like a puppy on its back. One arm is especially active . . . and curves up over its own body as if a dinosaur were looking behind him.

How slowly and evenly it moves! The starfish is a glacier, going sixty miles a year! It moves over the pink rock, by means I cannot see . . . and into marvelously floating delicate brown weeds. It is about the size of the bottom of a pail. When I reach out to it, it holds on firmly, and then slowly relaxes . . . I suddenly take an arm and lift it. The underside is a pale tan . . . gradually as I watch, thousands of tiny tubes begin rising from all over the underside . . . hundreds in the mouth, hundreds along the nineteen underarms . . . all looking . . . feeling . . . like a man looking for a woman . . . tiny heads blindly feeling for a rock and finding only air. A purple rim runs along the underside of every arm, with paler tubes. Probably its moving-feet. . . .

I put him back in . . . he unfolds—I had forgotten how purple he was—and slides down into his rock groin, the snail-like feelers waving as if nothing had happened, and nothing has.

Looking West from Laguna Beach at Night

Charles Wright

I've always liked the view from my mother-in-law's house at night,
Oil rigs off Long Beach
Like floating lanterns out in the smog-dark Pacific,
Stars in the eucalyptus,
Lights of airplanes arriving from Asia, and town lights
Littered like broken glass around the bay and back up the hill.

In summer, dance music is borne up
On the sea winds from the hotel's beach deck far below,
"Twist and Shout," or "Begin the Beguine."
It's nice to think that somewhere someone is having a good time,
And pleasant to picture them down there
Turned out, tipsy and flushed, in their white shorts and their
turquoise shirts.

Later, I like to sit and look up
At the mythic history of Western civilization,
Pinpricked and clued through the zodiac.
I'd like to be able to name them, say what's what and how who got
where,
Curry the physics of metamorphosis and its endgame,
But I've spent my life knowing nothing.

By the Pacific

Jessica Joyce

Exhausted from a week of work and PMS,
Thursday afternoon, the reports all written,
We drove north to a cabin near Point Reyes
Deeply in the spruce and alders hidden
And so peaceful when we closed the door,
We stripped naked and sat in a tub of hot water
In the twilight in sight of the Pacific shore,
Sat immersed and melted into each other,
Your pale cheek planted on my chest,
Naked and afloat in the twilight hush,
Warm and slippery as fish at rest,
No words spoken, only our nibbling lips and touch.
    Then the hot shower in the chilly air,
    Me scrubbing your back, your rump, your dark
brown hair.

Long Island Sound

Emma Lazarus

I see it as it looked one afternoon
In August,—by a fresh soft breeze o'erblown.
The swiftness of the tide, the light thereon,
A far-off sail, white as a crescent moon.
The shining waters with pale currents strewn,
The quiet fishing-smacks, the Eastern cove,
The semi-circle of its dark, green grove.
The luminous grasses, and the merry sun
In the grave sky; the sparkle far and wide,
Laughter of unseen children, cheerful chirp
Of crickets, and low lisp of rippling tide,
Light summer clouds fantastical as sleep
Changing unnoted while I gazed thereon.
All these fair sounds and sights I made my own.

Carmel Point

Robinson Jeffers

The extraordinary patience of things!
The beautiful place defaced with a crop of suburban houses—
How beautiful when we first beheld it,
Unbroken field of poppy and lupin walled with clean cliffs;
No intrusion but two or three horses pasturing,
Or a few milch cows rubbing their flanks on the outcrop rock-heads—
Now the spoiler has come: does it care?
Not faintly. It has all time. It knows the people are a tide
That swells and in time will ebb, and all
Their works dissolve. Meanwhile the image of the pristine beauty
Lives in the very grain of the granite,
Safe as the endless ocean that climbs our cliff.—As for us:
We must uncenter our minds from ourselves;
We must unhumanize our views a little, and become confident
As the rock and ocean that we were made from.

The Florida Beach

Constance Fenimore Woolson

Our drift-wood fire burns drowsily,
    The fog hangs low afar,
A thousand sea-birds fearlessly
    Hover above the bar;
Our boat is drawn far up the strand,
    Beyond the tide's long reach;
Like a fringe to the dark green winter land,
    Shines the silvery Florida beach.

Behind, the broad pine barrens lie
    Without a path or trail,
Before, the ocean meets the sky
    Without a rock or sail.
We call across to Africa,
    As a poet called to Spain:
A murmur of "Antony! Antony!"
    The waves bring back in refrain.

Far to the south the beach shines on,
    Dotted with giant shells;
Coral sprays from the white reef won,
    Radiate spiny cells;
Glass-like creatures that ride the waves,
    With azure sail and oar,
And wide-mouthed things from the deep sea caves
    That melt away on the shore.

Wild ducks gaze as we pass along:
       They have not learned to fear;
The mocking-bird keeps on his song
       In the low palmetto near;
The sluggish stream from the everglade
       Shows the alligator's track,
And the sea is broken in light and shade
       With the heave of the dolphin's back.

The Spanish light-house stands in haze:
       The keeper trims his light;
No sail he sees through the long, long days,
       No sail through the still, still night;
But ships that pass far out at sea,
       Along the warm Gulf Stream,
From Cuba and tropic Carribee,
       Keep watch for his distant gleam.

Alone, alone we wander on,
       In the southern winter day.
Through the dreamy veil the fog has spun
       The world seems far away;
The tide comes in—the birds fly low,
       As if to catch our speech.
Ah, Destiny! Why must we ever go
       Away from the Florida beach?

15

NEVER EXPECTED
TO BE THERE

Driving with Uncle Bailey

David Lee Garrison

Driving so slowly that a policeman
pulls him over and sniffs,
Uncle Bailey fumbles for his license,
then volunteers his social security card
and brags *I've been collecting*
benefits for over thirty years!

He survived the Depression
on his job as a rural postman,
now he jerks his old Ford to a stop
and rolls down the window
before he remembers
he has no mail to deliver.
Are you a Democrat or a Republican?
he asks, pretending
that he has halted to make sure
no liberals get a free ride.

Did I ever tell you I'm a war hero?
he laughs. Sworn in,
then discharged a few hours later
because World War I had ended,
he's the oldest veteran in the county,
grand marshal of the November parade.

Execution

Edward Hirsch

The last time I saw my high school football coach
He had cancer stenciled into his face
Like pencil marks from the sun, like intricate
Drawings on the chalkboard, small *x*'s and o's
That he copied down in a neat numerical hand
Before practice in the morning. By day's end
The board was a spiderweb of options and counters,
Blasts and sweeps, a constellation of players
Shining under his favorite word, *Execution*,
Underlined in the upper right-hand corner of things.
He believed in football like a new religion
And had perfect unquestioning faith in the fundamentals
Of blocking and tackling, the idea of warfare
Without suffering or death, the concept of teammates
Moving in harmony like the planets—and yet
Our awkward adolescent bodies were always canceling
The flawless beauty of Saturday afternoons in September,
Falling away from the particular grace of autumn,
The clear weather, the ideal game he imagined.
And so he drove us through punishing drills
On weekday afternoons, and doubled our practice time,
And challenged us to hammer him with forearms,
And devised elaborate, last-second plays—a flea-
Flicker, a triple reverse—to save us from defeat.
Almost always they worked. He despised losing
And loved winning more than his own body, maybe even

More than himself. But the last time I saw him
He looked wobbly and stunned by illness,
And I remembered the game in my senior year
When we met a downstate team who loved hitting
More than we did, who battered us all afternoon
With a vengeance, who destroyed us with timing
And power, with deadly, impersonal authority,
Machine-like fury, perfect execution.

Wagons

Maxine Kumin

Their wheelchairs are Conestoga wagons drawn
into the arc of a circle at 2 P.M.

Elsie, Gladys, Hazel, Fanny, Dora
whose names were coinage after the First World War

remember their parents tuned to the Fireside Chats,
remember in school being taught to hate the Japs.

They sit attentive as seals awaiting their fish
as the therapist sings out her cheerful directives:

Square the shoulders, lean back, straighten the knee
and lift! Tighten, lift and hold, Ladies!

They will retrain the side all but lost in a stroke,
the spinal cord mashed but not severed in traffic.

They will learn to adjust to their newly replaced
hips, they will walk on feet of shapely plastic.

This darling child in charge of their destiny
will lead them forward across the prairie.

Meadowbrook Nursing Home

Alice N. Persons

On our last visit, when Lucy was fifteen
and getting creaky herself,
one of the nurses said to me,
"Why don't you take the cat to Mrs. Harris' room
—poor thing lost her leg to diabetes last fall—
she's ninety, and blind, and no one comes to see her."

The door was open. I asked the tiny woman in the bed
if she would like me to bring Lucy in, and she turned her head
toward us. "Oh, yes, I want to touch her."

"I had a cat called Lily—she was so pretty, all white.
She was with me for twenty years, after my husband died too.
She slept with me every night—I loved her very much.
It's hard, in here, since I can't get around."

Lucy was settling in on the bed.
"You won't believe it, but I used to love to dance.
I was a fool for it! I even won contests.
I wish I had danced more.
It's funny, what you miss when everything . . . . . is gone."
This last was a murmur. She'd fallen asleep.

I lifted the cat
from the bed, tiptoed out, and drove home.
I tried to do some desk work
but couldn't focus.

I went downstairs, pulled the shades,
put on Tina Turner
and cranked it up loud
and I danced.
I danced.

Spring and All 1923

William Carlos Williams

I
By the road to the contagious hospital
under the surge of the blue
mottled clouds driven from the
northeast—a cold wind. Beyond, the
waste of broad, muddy fields
brown with dried weeds, standing and fallen

patches of standing water
the scattering of tall trees

All along the road the reddish
purplish, forked, upstanding, twiggy
stuff of bushes and small trees
with dead, brown leaves under them
leafless vines—

Lifeless in appearance, sluggish
dazed spring approaches—

They enter the new world naked,
cold, uncertain of all
save that they enter. All about them
the cold, familiar wind—

Now the grass, tomorrow
the stiff curl of wildcarrot leaf

One by one objects are defined—
It quickens: clarity, outline of leaf

But now the stark dignity of
entrance—Still, the profound change
has come upon them: rooted, they
grip down and begin to awaken

At Summerford's Nursing Home

Rodney Jones

Like plants in pots, they sit along the wall,
Breached at odd angles, wheelchairs locked,
Or drift in tortoise-calm ahead of doting sons:

Some are still continent and wink at others
Who seem to float in and out of being here,
And one has balked beside the check-in desk—

A jaunty shred of carrot glowing on one lip,
He fumbles a scared hug from each little girl
Among the carolers from the Methodist church

Until two nurses shush him and move him on.
There is a snatch of sermon from the lounge,
And then my fourth-grade teacher washes up,

And someone else—who is it?—nodding the pale
Varicose bloom of his skull: the bald postman,
The butcher from our single grocery store?

Or is that me, graft on another forty years?
Will I become that lump, attached to tubes
That pump in mush and drain the family money?

Or will I be the one who stops it with a gun,
Or, more insensibly, with pills and alcohol?
And would it be so wrong to liberate this one

Who stretches toward me from his bed and moans
Above the constant chlorine of cleaning up
When from farther down the hall I hear the first

Transmogrifying groans: the bestial O and O
Repeating like a mantra that travels long
Roads of nerves to move a sound that comes

And comes but won't come finally up to words,
Not the oldest ones that made the stories go,
Not even *love*, or *help*, or *hurt*, but goodbye

And hello, grandfather, the rest of your life
Coiled around you like a rope, while one by
One, we strange relatives lean to be recognized.

Earl

Louis Jenkins

In Sitka, because they are fond of them,
people have named the seals. Every seal
is named Earl because they are killed one
after another by the orca, the killer
whale; seal bodies tossed left and right
into the air. "At least he didn't get
Earl," someone says. And sure enough,
after a time, that same friendly,
bewhiskered face bobs to the surface.
It's Earl again. Well, how else are you
to live except by denial, by some
palatable fiction, some little song to
sing while the inevitable, the black and
white blindsiding fact, comes hurtling
toward you out of the deep?

His Stillness

Sharon Olds

The doctor said to my father, "You asked me
to tell you when nothing more could be done.
That's what I'm telling you now." My father
sat quite still, as he always did,
especially not moving his eyes. I had thought
he would rave if he understood he would die,
wave his arms and cry out. He sat up,
thin, and clean, in his clean gown,
like a holy man. The doctor said,
"There are things we can do which might give you time,
but we cannot cure you." My father said,
"Thank you." And he sat, motionless, alone,
with the dignity of a foreign leader.
I sat beside him. This was my father.
He had known he was mortal. I had feared they would have to
tie him down. I had not remembered
he had always held still and kept quiet to bear things,
the liquor a way to keep still. I had not
known him. My father had dignity. At the
end of his life his life began
to wake in me.

Still Life in Landscape

Sharon Olds

It was night, it had rained, there were pieces of cars and
half-cars strewn, it was still, and bright,
a woman was lying on the highway, on her back,
with her head curled back and tucked under her shoulders
so the back of her head touched her spine
between her shoulder blades, her clothes
mostly accidented off, and her
leg gone, a tall bone
sticking out of the stub of her thigh—
this was her abandoned matter,
my mother grabbed my head and turned it and
clamped it into her chest, between
her breasts. My father was driving—not sober
but not in this accident, we'd approached it out of
neutral twilight, broken glass
on wet black macadam, an underlying
midnight abristle with stars. This was
the world—maybe the only one.
The dead woman was not the person
my father had recently almost run over,
who had suddenly leapt away from our family
car, jerking back from death,
she was not I, she was not my mother,
but maybe she was a model of the mortal,
the elements ranged around her on the tar—
glass, bone, metal, flesh, and the family.

The Slave Auction

Frances Ellen Watkins Harper

The sale began—young girls were there,
   Defenceless in their wretchedness,
Whose stifled sobs of deep despair
   Revealed their anguish and distress.

And mothers stood, with streaming eyes,
   And saw their dearest children sold;
Unheeded rose their bitter cries,
   While tyrants barter'd them for gold.

And woman, with her love and truth—
   For these in sable forms may dwell—
Gaz'd on the husband of her youth,
   With anguish none may paint or tell.

And men, whose sole crime was their hue,
   The impress of their Maker's hand,
And frail and shrinking children too,
   Were gathered in that mournful band.

Ye who have laid your lov'd to rest,
   And wept above their lifeless clay,
Know not the anguish of that breast,
   Whose lov'd are rudely torn away.

Ye may not know how desolate
   Are bosoms rudely forced to part,
And how a dull and heavy weight
   Will press the life-drops from the heart.

There's been a Death, in the Opposite House

Emily Dickinson

There's been a Death, in the Opposite House,
As lately as Today—
I know it, by the numb look
Such Houses have—alway—

The Neighbors rustle in and out—
The Doctor—drives away—
A Window opens like a Pod—
Abrupt—mechanically—

Somebody flings a Mattress out—
The Children hurry by—
They wonder if it died—on that—
I used to—when a Boy—

The Minister—goes stiffly in—
As if the House were His—
And he owned all the Mourners—now—
And little Boys—besides—

And then the Milliner—and the Man
Of the Appalling Trade—
To take the measure of the House—
There'll be that Dark Parade—

Of Tassels—and of Coaches—soon—
It's easy as a Sign—
The Intuition of the News—
In just a Country Town—

the hookers, the madmen and the doomed

Charles Bukowski

today at the track
2 or 3 days after
the death of the
jock
came this voice
over the speaker
asking us all to stand
and observe
a few moments
of silence. well,
that's a tired
formula and
I don't like it
but I do like
silence. so we
all stood: the
hookers and the
madmen and the
doomed. I was
set to be dis-
pleased but then
I looked up at the
TV screen
and there
standing silently
in the paddock

waiting to mount
up
stood the other jocks
along with
the officials and
the trainers:
quiet and thinking
of death and the
one gone,
they stood
in a semi-circle
the brave little
men in boots and
silks,
the legions of death
appeared and
vanished, the sun
blinked once
I thought of love
with its head ripped
off
still trying to
sing and
then the announcer
said, thank you
and we all went on about
our business.

The Edward C. Peterson Tree

Charlie Langdon

In Scipio, Utah, Millard County,
the boys go barefoot still and play under
trees in the park. Teenage girls ride horseback
on Main Street while lambs prance along behind,
We lunched there one Saturday and watched them
and petted their round puppy with no tail.
Go there now, if you care to, and see them.
And there you'll also find a tree behind
a fence, a splayed two-trunked tree planted
long ago in memory of Edward
C. Peterson, who died on the last day
of the First World War in 1918.
"Edward C. Peterson," the plaque read, "killed
In the Argonne, November eleven."
November eleven! To die that day,
to lose your life as the guns fell silent
in the eleventh hour, eleventh day,
eleventh month, oh what a riddle fate.
And what a riddle question, what is war
or peace, life or death? Something or nothing?
Convened wisdom would weep under that tree
and all sages fall silent in its shade.
In Scipio, Utah, Millard County,
the boys go barefoot still and play under
trees in the park. Teenage girls ride horseback.
Go there now, anytime now, and see them.

Safe in their Alabaster Chambers

Emily Dickinson

Safe in their Alabaster Chambers—
Untouched by Morning—
And untouched by Noon—
Lie the meek members of the Resurrection—
Rafter of Satin—and Roof of Stone!

Grand go the Years—in the Crescent—above them—
Worlds scoop their Arcs—
And Firmaments—row—
Diadems—drop—and Doges—surrender—
Soundless as dots—on a Disc of Snow—

Grandma's Grave

Freya Manfred

Mother and I brush long drifts of snow from the gravestones
of my great grandfather and grandmother, great uncle and aunt,
two of mother's brothers, each less than a year old,
and her last-born brother, George Shorba, dead at sixteen:
> *1925–1942*
> *A Mastermind. My Beloved Son.*

But we can't find the grave of Grandma, who buried all the rest.

Mother stands dark-browed and musing, under the pines,
and I imagine her as a child, wondering why her mother
left home so often to tend the sick, the dying, the dead.
Borrowing a shovel, she digs, until she uncovers:
> *1889–1962*
> *Mary Shorba*

Mother almost never cries, but she does now. She stares
at this stone as if it were the answer to all the hidden things.

It Was a Normal Day Except I Fell

Julie Sheehan

At 9:47 leaping, leaving the 108th floor, impressive
      to walk-up buddies,
         nothing quite like it in the Bronx:
Farewell, and 103rd floor, too, and there's Jerome, farewell,
      another scholarship kid;
On the elevator of public opinion, Raymond saying
        you're headed up, my man,
            up!
My own brother, who always sank the hook shot,
The back-home necks craning, tenements craning at my visits,
      my strides;

Farewell, 84th, and 54th, cell phones and land lines ringing,
      the whole hive on the hook with their homes,
      saying (I said it, too) *I love you, I'm okay,*
Farewell last words, preprogrammed at our unpacking,
      good taste in the mouth of survival,
      even the bullies found you.

Farewell, second-best khakis, the creases I love hardwired,
         constructive,
      under the dry cleaner's diaphanous hygiene,
And best of luck, closet, my secrets, my order:
Your cotton pinstripes ballooning and shrill
      sing me down, whistle me,
      flap as I flap, pure folly,

Ah, the sky so blue, the sun in plain view, the cool
 silver siding, the heat inside—
I, no Icarus, no hubris, small pride in small mercies,
Farewell me, expanding like heat, my bones
Buckling, O Mother, O Father I never knew, O Love,
 what have we here?

Sweet Annie Divine

Corey Mesler

Sweet Annie Divine (1925–1976). Born Rooster, Arkansas, Annie
May Auspex. Also known as The Duchess. Dropped out of school
at the age of 13 to work her parents' cotton fields. Started singing
professionally at 16 in juke joints in Arkansas, Mississippi and
Tennessee. Toured with Jimmy Reed for a while, sang with Styx
Ygg's BamBam Five on Beale Street in the forties. Fronted her own
band, The Moxie Seven (or Eight depending on the night), which
included Hillbilly Thomas and Sweetie Sykes and they had a
mid-major hit with "Stephen Daedalus's Blues" in 1948. Recorded
"Chicken Finger Blues," "Write Em Right," "Saint Ursula Goes
Down for the Third Time," and her signature tune "Mississippi
Low-down Blues" for the Lightning Label. She is credited with
the composition of only one standard, the rocking "Lemme Get
Up First," later, of course, covered by The Rolling Stones. Her
last record for a major label was a cover of Holmes and Howard's
"Somebody's Been Using that Thing." Comparisons to Big Mama
Thornton and Bessie Smith brought her a brief renaissance of
interest in the restless sixties. She died of the drink in a Memphis
boarding house, just hours after recording her last record, the
plaintive and pain-filled "I'm a Drunk in a Memphis Boarding
House." Alan Lomax has said of her, "She could have been one
of the greats if not for the hooch."

Dedication for a Plot of Ground

William Carlos Williams

This plot of ground
facing the waters of this inlet
is dedicated to the living presence of
Emily Richardson Wellcome
who was born in England; married;
lost her husband and with
her five year old son
sailed for New York in a two-master;
was driven to the Azores;
ran adrift on Fire Island shoal,
met her second husband
in a Brooklyn boarding house,
went with him to Puerto Rico
bore three more children, lost
her second husband, lived hard
for eight years in St. Thomas,
Puerto Rico, San Domingo, followed
the oldest son to New York,
lost her daughter, lost her "baby,"
seized the two boys of
the oldest son by the second marriage
mothered them—they being
motherless—fought for them
against the other grandmother
and the aunts, brought them here
summer after summer, defended
herself here against thieves,

storms, sun, fire,
against flies, against girls
that came smelling about, against
drought, against weeds, storm-tides,
neighbors, weasels that stole her chickens,
against the weakness of her own hands,
against the growing strength of
the boys, against wind, against
the stones, against trespassers,
against rents, against her own mind.

She grubbed this earth with her own hands,
domineered over this grass plot,
blackguarded her oldest son
into buying it, lived here fifteen years,
attained a final loneliness and—

If you can bring nothing to this place
but your carcass, keep out.

On the Road to Woodlawn

Theodore Roethke

I miss the polished brass, the powerful black horses,
The drivers creaking the seats of the baroque hearses,
The high-piled floral offerings with sentimental verses,
The carriages reeking with varnish and stale perfume.
I miss the pallbearers momentously taking their places,
The undertaker's obsequious grimaces,
The craned necks, the mourners' anonymous faces,
—And the eyes, still vivid, looking up from a sunken room.

Biographies

Virginia Hamilton ADAIR (1913–2004, Bronx, NY) grew up an only child in Montclair, NJ, wrote her first poem at age six, and won prizes for her poetry at Mount Holyoke, but after she got married she stopped trying to get her poems published, though she continued to write them for almost 50 years. After her children had grown, her husband had died, and she lost her eyesight, she finally published her first book of poems, *Ants on the Melon* (1996), when she was 83. She went on to publish two more books: *Beliefs and Blasphemies* (1998) and *Living on Fire* (2000). *Publishing takes a sort of canniness that I didn't really think went with poetry. I was afraid of writing to please somebody else instead of myself.*

Rick AGRAN (1960) grew up in Brookline, NH. He lives near there now, at the foot of Blue Job Mountain. When he was 20, he read Jack Kerouac's *On the Road* (he and Kerouac share a birthday: March 12) and that summer he hitchhiked 10,000 miles and wound up in Seattle, where he sold jewelry and hawked fresh vegetables and cheese in Pike Place Market. He's worked as a cook, dishwasher, woodcutter, and teacher of writing.

Debra ALLBERY (1957, Lancaster, OH) is the director of the Warren Wilson MFA Program for Writers. *Poems are made the way that paintings are made, involving juxtaposition, balance, a directing of the eye.*

Ellen BASS (1947, Philadelphia) has written poetry and several books of nonfiction to support and guide GLBT youth (*Free Your Mind*) and adult survivors of childhood sexual abuse (*Beginning to Heal* and *Courage to Heal*).

Jeffrey BEAN (1978) grew up in Bloomington, IN, majored in music at Oberlin College, and his debut collection of poetry, *Diminished Fifth*, reflects on the power of music in a merciless world. He teaches English at Central Michigan University. *I love reading literary magazines. I collect them like comic books. I love the way they smell.*

June BEISCH (1939–2010, Ashland, WI) grew up in Minneapolis, where her father died when she was young. She later wrote:

> *Welfare children, we were wary of luxury,*
> *distrustful of those bearing gifts.*

She went to New York, became an actress and model, married, lived in London, San Francisco, and Cambridge, had two children, took up freelance writing, and then started writing poetry at 43, a few years after she was diagnosed with breast cancer, and lived to the age of 70.

Wendell BERRY (1934, Port Royal, KY) is a sixth-generation farmer who grew up learning how to hitch mules. He left Port Royal for college and to live in California and Italy and teach at Stanford and NYU, and then, in 1964, he went back to farm the hill country where he was born, 250 acres along the Kentucky River near where it flows into the Ohio, with his wife, Tanya, and grow squash, corn, and tomatoes, and tend sheep, a milk cow, and some horses. *We learn from our gardens to deal with the most urgent question of the time: How much is enough?*

George BILGERE (1951, St. Louis) was an actor and producer for NHK television in Tokyo and lived in Spain for a year on a Fulbright. He teaches in Cleveland and spends the summers writing in Berlin.

Michael BLUMENTHAL (1949) graduated from Cornell Law School, was director of creative writing at Harvard, and now teaches law at West Virginia University. A frequent translator from German, French, and Hungarian, he spends summers in a small village near the shores of Lake Balaton in Hungary.

Robert BLY (1926, Madison, MN) was the son of Norwegian farmers *(I tried to become a playwright . . . the trouble was that nobody in my family talked)* who, after the Navy and Harvard, spent three years living down and out in New York, taking odd jobs as a file clerk or painter, sleeping in Grand Central when necessary, writing 12 hours a day. Determined to stay clear of universities, having discovered the work of Pablo Neruda, César Vallejo, Georg Trakl, and other major poets little known in literary academia, he moved back to Minnesota in 1955, to a farm near his parents', and he set out to promote foreign poets (and to insult the great sacred elephants of American lit) in his magazine *The Fifties*, which became *The Sixties* and then *The Seventies*. His *Silence in the Snowy Fields* came out in 1962. A prolific writer and translator and editor and performer at workshops, he burst into best-sellerdom in 1990 with *Iron John: A Book About Men*, a treatise on the Grimm Brothers fairy tale. *One day while studying a Yeats poem I decided to write poetry the rest of my life. I recognized that a single short poem has room for history, music, psychology, religious thought, mood, occult speculation, character, and events of one's own life.*

Laure-Anne BOSSELAAR (1943) grew up in Belgium, where she worked in radio and television, and moved to the United States in 1987 to enroll in an MFA program. She translates American poetry into French and Flemish poetry into English and is part of the faculty of Pine Manor College in Chestnut Hill, MA.

Jon BOWERMAN (1938, Medford, OR) is a horse trainer and working cowboy, whose great-grandfather, Thomas B. Hoover, founded the town of Fossil, OR, in 1876. His father, Bill Bowerman, was the cofounder of Nike. Jon lives on a ranch outside of Fossil.

Marcia F. BROWN (1953, Bradford, MA) grew up taking ballet and piano lessons and singing in the church choir and then took up poetry in college. She got a theater degree and moved to New York in 1975 and ended up working as an assistant, a secretary, and as a film and television editor. In 1984 she moved to Portland, ME, and started work as a developer of low-income rental housing. She lives with her husband on a farm on the coast of Maine.

Philip BRYANT (1951, Chicago) grew up on Chicago's South Side and hung out at a record store called Blues and the Abstract Truth, listening to jazz. He collaborated with jazz pianist Carolyn Wilkins on *Stompin' at the Grand Terrace: A Jazz Memoir in Verse*. *The first real poetry I heard early on was Shakespeare. My mother read the plays aloud to my sister and me.*

David BUDBILL (1940, Cleveland) has worked as a carpenter's apprentice, short-order cook, coffeehouse manager, day laborer, forester, gardener, pastor of a church, and college instructor. He lives in the mountains of northern Vermont with his wife in a house they built themselves.

Charles BUKOWSKI (1920–1994) grew up unhappy in Los Angeles, a little kid with severe acne, a target for bullies. He wrote stories, was published at 24, got discouraged, slipped into 10 years of heavy drinking. After a near-fatal ulcer, he started writing poetry again. *This is very important—to take leisure time. Pace is the essence. There have to be great pauses between highs, where you do nothing at all. You just lay on a bed and stare at the ceiling.*

Reid BUSH is a poet, gardener, retired teacher, and daily writer living in Louisville, KY.

Julie CADWALLADER-STAUB (1957, Minneapolis) grew up with five sisters, married her college roommate's older brother, had three children, and moved to Vermont, where she works for the Burlington school district.

Gabrielle CALVOCORESSI (1974) grew up in central Connecticut, where her family owned several small-town movie theaters. When she was 13, her mother took her own life. She lives in Los Angeles and is the author of *The Last Time I Saw Amelia Earhart* and *Apocalyptic Swing*. *For me, writing and prayer are not so different . . . I don't expect an answer when I pray.*

Raymond CARVER (1938–1988, Clatskanie, OR) grew up in Yakima, WA, among hardworking, hard-drinking people in a poor neighborhood known as "the hole." He had a wife and two children by the time he was 20, took jobs as a janitor, sawmill worker, deliveryman, went to college, worked as a night custodian, wrote during the day, and got his break in 1967 with his short story "Will You Please Be Quiet, Please?" He drank heavily, and then quit in 1977 after nearly dying, and married the poet Tess Gallagher. He stayed sober for 11 years, dying of lung cancer, at age 50, in Port Angeles, WA, where he lies in a grave overlooking the Strait of Juan de Fuca. *I'm prouder of that, that I've quit drinking, than I am of anything in my life.*

Johnny CASH (1932–2003) was born in Kingsland, AR, and worked on the family cotton farm alongside his parents, Ray and Carrie, and six siblings. He served in the U.S. Air Force, had eight *Billboard* country hits between 1984 and 2003, and survived years of addiction to narcotics. The year before he died he recorded *American IV: The Man Comes Around* with producer Rick Rubin.

Michael CHITWOOD (1958, Rocky Mount, VA) was a freelance science writer and now teaches at the University of North Carolina in Chapel Hill.

Amy M. CLARK (1966, Minneapolis) grew up in San Luis Obispo, CA, went back to Minnesota to attend Carleton College, then returned to the West Coast to teach English and got into publishing. She lives in Concord, MA, where she is a freelance writer and editor.

Billy COLLINS (1941, New York, NY) published his first book, *The Apple That Astonished Paris*, when he was 47. His *Sailing Alone Around the Room* (2000) sold a couple hundred thousand copies, which is huge in poetry publishing. Noting that modern poetry lacks humor, he said: *"It's the fault of the Romantics, who eliminated humor from poetry. Shakespeare's hilarious, Chaucer's hilarious. The Romantics killed off humor, and they also eliminated sex, things which were replaced by landscape. I thought that was a pretty bad trade-off, so I'm trying to write about humor and landscape, and occasionally sex."*

Matt COOK (1969, Milwaukee, WI) is a slam poet, author of *The Unreasonable Slug, Eavesdrop Soup,* and *In the Small of My Backyard. It was easy to write the Great American Novel when there were only five American Novels.*

Nancy Vieira COUTO (1942, New Bedford, MA) studied at Cornell and is the author of *The Face in the Water* (1990). She lives in Ithaca.

Barbara CROOKER (1945, Cold Spring, NY) started writing poetry in her late 20s, as a single mother. "VCCA" in her poem refers to the Virginia Center for the Creative Arts, a colony for artists and writers in Sweet Briar, VA. *I write in longhand with a pen (a black-ink roller ball—it has to be black), on a lined yellow pad. I start out in longhand drafts because I want the physical connection, from the mind to the hand to the page.*

Cortney DAVIS (1945, Easton, MD) is a nurse practitioner in Redding, CT. *I write from the nurse's vantage point: we accompany patients as they go from illness to recovery; we walk with patients as they journey through death's door.*

Kate DiCAMILLO (1964, Philadelphia, PA) grew up in Clermont, FL, now lives in Minneapolis and writes two pages a day, five days a week. *E.B. White said, "All that I hope to say in books, all that I ever hope to say, is that I love the world." That's the way I feel too.*

Emily DICKINSON (1830–1886) was born in Amherst, MA, and lived there all her life, except for a year attending Mount Holyoke (where she was the only student unwilling to publicly confess faith in Christ) and brief trips to Boston, Philadelphia, and Washington. A lively, sociable young woman, she became more reclusive, while composing 1,755 brief lyrics on scraps of paper (most of them during the years of the Civil War), which she kept secret even from her family, hiding them in bureau drawers. She died of nephritis, an inflammation of the kidneys. Her last words: "I must go in, for the fog is rising." *People need hard times and oppression to develop psychic muscles.*

Kirsten DIERKING (1962, Minneapolis, MN) was in real estate before she got into teaching and writing poetry.

Gregory DJANIKIAN (1949, Alexandria, Egypt) is the son of Armenian parents who moved to the United States when he was 8. He lives near Philadelphia, where he directs the creative writing program at the University of Pennsylvania.

Susan DONNELLY (1939) was born and raised near Boston in a large Irish-American extended family. After college she lived in Manhattan for several years, working in offices and relying on programs in arts centers and colonies to practice her writing. Her latest book is *Capture the Flag* (2009). She lives in Cambridge, MA, and teaches poetry from her home.

Stephen DUNN (1939, New York) was a star on the 1962 Hofstra basketball team (25–1) nicknamed "Radar" for his jump shot. He played pro ball for a year, went to work at Nabisco as a copywriter, and wrote fiction in his spare time, then poetry. He quit Nabisco to spend a year in Spain, then grad school. *Once, my silence possessed me. Now that I possess it, I'd like to learn to better let it find its necessary speech.*

Ralph Waldo EMERSON (1803–1882) was a Boston clergyman who left the pulpit after three years to become a public lecturer, one of the first ever to make his living on the lecture circuit, giving three or four a week at $100 apiece, traveling by train ("A man writes a lecture, & is carted round the Country at the tail of his lecture, for months, to read it.") as far west as St. Louis, earning in a month what a minister earned in a year. *Meek young men grow up in libraries, believing it their duty to accept the views, which Cicero, which Locke, which Bacon, have given, forgetful that Cicero, Locke, and Bacon were only young men in libraries, when they wrote those books.*

Patricia FARGNOLI (1937, Hartford, CT) is a retired psychotherapist with a background in social work who lives in Walpole, NH. *My ideal readers are "townspeople," . . . ordinary people who will see themselves and their own worlds in what I write. I want my poems to be a bridge between us.*

Lawrence FERLINGHETTI (1919, Yonkers, NY) served in World War II, settled in San Francisco, and opened City Lights Bookstore, which published Allen Ginsberg's "Howl" and, later, Ferlinghetti's *A Coney Island of the Mind*, a bestselling book of the Sixties. *Poetry is the shadow cast by our streetlight imaginations.*

Edward FIELD (1924, Brooklyn, NY) served in World War II as a navigator in heavy bombers and flew 25 missions over Germany. He studied at NYU and lives in New York City, where he wrote *The Man Who Would Marry Susan Sontag and*

Other Intimate Literary Portraits of the Bohemian Era. Poetry is no different than newspapers. What you think about is what you should write about.

James FINNEGAN (1955) lives in West Hartford, CT, a banking insurance underwriter. He runs an Internet discussion listserv called the NewPoetry List, a blog called Ursprache, and LitStation, a poetry Web radio project. *Poetry presupposes its own purpose.*

Chris FORHAN (1959, Seattle, WA) was a TV news director in Great Falls, MT, until, at 40, he went back to grad school for his MFA.

Sarah FRELIGH (1951, Adrian, MI) wrote sports for *The Philadelphia Inquirer.* She wrote a baseball novel in verse, *Sort of Gone.* She lives and teaches in Rochester, NY. *Although I'd like to think that "poem" is not a four-letter word, to most people it probably is an obscenely elitist pastime. But I also think that good writing, whatever the genre, starts with reportage; that is, observing the world around you and translating it for your audience through your own unique filter.*

David Lee GARRISON (1945, Bremerton, WA) lives in Dayton, OH, and teaches Spanish and Portuguese at Wright State University.

Deborah GARRISON (1965, Ann Arbor) went to Brown, edited fiction at *The New Yorker,* lives with her husband and children in Montclair, NJ, and is an editor at Knopf and Pantheon. *When I was unhappy / words slipped ceaselessly / from my pen, / arrows down the page, / tears run together, / running to tell.*

Dobby GIBSON (1970, Minneapolis) began writing poetry as a distraction from a novel he was working on. He has since abandoned fiction. He wrote his first book of poems, *Polar,* while working 60 hours a week at a corporate job. *I discovered I loved poetry around the same time I discovered I loved indie rock.*

Allen GINSBERG (1926–1997, Newark, NJ). His father was a high school English teacher and poet. His mother, who suffered from recurrent seizures and paranoia, often took Allen and his brother, Eugene, to meetings of the Communist Party-USA during the 1930s. She died in 1956 in a mental hospital. At Columbia University Ginsberg met the writers who would eventually call themselves the "Beat Generation." He became active in politics in the late 1960s and helped found the Jack Kerouac School of Disembodied Poetics at Naropa. He died of liver cancer at his home in the East Village, New York City.

Dana GIOIA (1950, Los Angeles, CA), of Italian and Mexican ancestry, studied at Harvard, went into business, then quit to be a writer. He has written two opera libretti and translates poetry from Latin, Italian, and German. He served two terms as chairman of the National Endowment for the Arts and left that position in 2009.

Natalie GOLDBERG (1948) is a teacher, painter, author of 11 books, and student of Zen Buddhism who made a documentary film—*Tangled Up In Bob*—about Bob Dylan. She lives in northern New Mexico. *Wild mind isn't just your mind; it's the whole world moving through you. With it, you give voice to a very large life, even though you might only be talking about your grandmother's closet with its particular wallpaper and floor. It's an awareness of everything through one thing.*

Charles GOODRICH (1951) has worked as a correctional work crew supervisor, a short-order cook, a carpenter, and a Zen gardener, and wrote a book of prose poems about gardening, *Going to Seed*. He lives and gardens in Corvallis, OR.

Alvin GREENBERG (1932, Cincinnati, OH) lives in Boise, ID, is the author of four novels, four collections of short stories, two books of nonfiction, and 10 volumes of poetry.

Linda GREGG (1942, Suffern, NY) grew up in Marin County, CA. She lives in New York and teaches at Princeton.

John HAAG (1926–2008) served four years in the Merchant Marines in World War II. He studied in England on a Fulbright and taught English at Penn State University.

John HAINES (1924, Norfolk, VA) served in the Navy during World War II and spent more than 20 years homesteading in Alaska, in a modest cabin that he built himself. He was a painter who switched to writing because painting was too hard during the Alaska winter. He lives in Fairbanks. *I think that we get more and more impoverished as a consequence of technology—the ease which makes it possible to put something down instantly on a piece of paper or on a screen or whatever. But something gets lost.*

Donald HALL (1928, New Haven) was hooked on Poe as a boy: *I wanted to be mad, addicted, obsessed, haunted, and cursed; I wanted to have eyes that burned like coals, profoundly melancholy, profoundly attractive.* The first poem he ever wrote was about death, and he gave it to his babysitter hoping to impress her. Hall felt most at home on his grandfather's New Hampshire farm, Eagle Pond, where the boy loved *"watching him milk his Holsteins as his dear voice kept time with his hands and he crooned wonderful bad poems with the elocutionary zeal of another century."* In 1975, Eagle Pond Farm pulled him back home, along with his wife, the late poet Jane Kenyon. He still lives and works there, writing about love, death, and New Hampshire. *I try every day to write great poetry as I tried when I was fourteen . . . What else is there to do?*

Barbara HAMBY (1952, New Orleans) was raised in Hawaii. She lives in Tallahassee and teaches at Florida State. *I grew up in a big talking family, so words have always been important to me. Both my mother and father were quick with a quip, and my mother, especially, used a lot of Biblical language. For instance, when I'd be fuming about how I wanted to kill my brother, she'd often say, "Vengeance is mine, sayeth the Lord." I can remember having half a dozen minor aneurysms when she'd come up with that or, "Vanity, vanity, all is vanity." She was an Old Testament gal and really dug Jehovah, because he kicked some serious ass.*

Patricia HAMPL (1946, St. Paul) is the daughter of a florist and a librarian. As a young girl, she wrote letters for her Czech grandmother, who could not write in English, often inserting her own poetic language and observations. She was educated in a convent by nuns, studied piano performance before majoring in English, and lives in St. Paul, not far from where she grew up. *My grandmother, when she served dinner, was a virtuoso hanging on the edge of her own ecstatic performance. She was a little power crazed: she had us and, by God, we were going to eat. The futility of saying no was supreme, and no one ever tried it. How could a son-in-law, already weakened by the once, twice, thrice charge to the barricades of pork and mashed potato, be expected to gather his feeble wit long enough to ignore the final call of his old commander when she sounded the alarm: "Pie, Fred?"*

W. C. HANDY (1873–1958, Florence, AL) grew up in a devout church family and joined a blues band secretly, then a traveling minstrel troupe, moved to Memphis in 1909 and set up shop on Beale Street. He worked the rest of his life composing, compiling, and publishing blues music.

Phebe HANSON (1928, Sacred Heart, MN) is the child of Norwegian immigrants. She has taught high school, college, and Sunday school classes and has kept a daily journal since 1941.

C.G. HANZLICEK (1942, Owatonna, MN) is the author of eight books of poetry. He taught at California State University, Fresno, for 35 years before retiring in 2001.

Frances Ellen Watkins HARPER (1825–1911, Baltimore) was an African American activist born to free parents and helped slaves escape along the Underground Railroad. After the Civil War, she toured the South speaking about reconstruction and education.

Jim HARRISON (1937, Grayling, MI) is the son of a county ag agent. When he was a child, while playing, his left eye was cut and he lost sight in it. *(Ever since I was seven and had my eye put out, I'd turn for solace to rivers, rain, trees, birds, lakes, animals.)* He went to Michigan State, taught in New York, moved back to Michigan, took a job as a construction worker. He wrote poetry and a few unsuccessful novels before *Legends of the Fall* (1979), which was made into a movie. *I'm a poet and we tend to err on the side that life is more than it appears rather than less.*

Robert HASS (1941, San Francisco) teaches at the University of California, Berkeley. *Everyone . . . wants to say in their own terms what it means to be alive. Poetry is the most common way, because the material of poetry is the stream of language that is constantly going on in our heads. It's very low tech. Anyone can do it.*

Linda M. HASSELSTROM (1943, TX) conducts writing retreats on the ranch in western South Dakota homesteaded by her grandfather in 1899. Her books of poetry include *Dakota Bones* and *Bitter Creek Junction*. www.windbreakhouse.com. *I love the wide land, the independence, even the occasional harshness of the prairies.*

Tom HENNEN (1942, Morris, MN) is a former park ranger and poet.

Nancy HENRY (1961, Chipley, FL) lives in Westbrook, ME, and is an attorney specializing in product liability and medical malpractice cases. With fellow law student Alice Persons, she founded Moon Pie Press in 2003. *Poetry and the community of poets . . . these have been my refuge and retreat from the painful parts of the practice of law. Poetry has also offered me a liberating, healing way to process and gain perspective on the legal work and sometimes to take potshots at the profession.*

Edward HIRSCH (1950, Chicago) has a Ph.D. in folklore and is the president of the John Simon Guggenheim Memorial Foundation. *Poetry never loses its* appeal. *Sometimes its audience wanes and sometimes it swells like a wave. But the essential mystery of being human is always going to engage and compel us. We're involved in a mystery. Poetry uses words to put us in touch with that mystery. We're always going to need it.*

John HOLLANDER (1929, New York City), the son of a research physiologist, attended the Bronx High School of Science, then Columbia. He has written liner notes for classical music albums and collaborated with composers on operatic and lyric works. He teaches at Yale. *I want my poems to be wiser than I am, to know more about themselves than I do.*

Bill HOLM (1943–2009) lived in Minneota, MN, and in Iceland, taught college English for many years in Marshall, played piano, organ, and harpsichord, a tall white-haired red-faced poet and prophet who collapsed in the Sioux Falls airport coming home from Patagonia, and died. *For it is life we want. We want the world, the whole beautiful world, alive—and we alive in it. That is the actual god we long for and seek, yet we have already found it, if we open our senses, our whole bodies, thus our souls. That is why I have written, and intend to continue, until someone among you takes up the happy work of keeping the chain letter of the soul moving along into whatever future will come.*

Garrett HONGO (1951, Volcano, HI) was born in the back room of his grandfather's general store. His family left for Southern California when he was a small boy, and when he returned thirty years later, he was recognized immediately as his father's son. *My concerns as a poet have to do not so much with emotional authenticity, but with emotional nobility—the idea that poems might help produce and reveal our better nature. It is an idea present in Oriental philosophy. I do want things to be better somehow, at least within myself, so that I might be more like the stillness that smoothes the surface of a pond rather than the bullfrog that jumps into it.*

Marie HOWE (1950, Rochester, NY) is the eldest daughter in a family of nine children. She lost her brother John to AIDS in 1989, and his *"living and dying changed my aesthetic completely."* Her second book of poems, *What the Living Do*, arose out of that loss. She lives in New York City with her daughter. *I feel like poets and writers are the monks writing illuminated manuscripts, in the sense of trying to preserve the integrity of language, just to expand the possibilities for expression, because the culture is trying to push us into the same twenty words over and over again.*

David HUDDLE (1942, Ivanhoe, VA) served in the U.S. Army in Germany and Vietnam. He taught at the University of Vermont from 1971 until he retired in 2009.

Robinson JEFFERS (1887–1962, Pittsburgh) was the son of a Presbyterian minister. He inherited enough money to devote himself to writing poetry and from 1924 until he died, he lived in seclusion by the ocean near Carmel, CA, in a stone house he had built himself.

Louis JENKINS (1942, Oklahoma City) lives in Duluth, MN. *All poetry, I think, comes down to storytelling. This is what happened. This is what it's like to be a live human being. You tell that story the best way you can.*

Rodney JONES (1950, Falkville, AL) grew up on a cotton farm four miles from a town of 400 that didn't get electricity until Jones was five or six years old, and where *"horses passed in front of [his] house every day."* He teaches English at Southern Illinois University at Carbondale. *I'm against all the games that might be played in a poem like "guess what's behind my back." Everything I do in a poem can be seen.*

Donald JUSTICE (1925–2004) grew up in Miami during the Depression, an only child of hardworking Southern Baptists, his father an itinerant carpenter, but his parents made sure their boy learned to play the piano. (He wrote about it in *The Sunset Maker: Poems/Stories/A Memoir* and about his piano teacher, Mrs. Snow, who "loomed above us like an alp, / We little towns below could feel her shadow. / Somehow her nods of approval seemed to matter / More than the stray flakes drifting from her scalp.") *It was clear to everyone, themselves included, that [the piano teachers] were dedicated less to teaching than to the small sums their teaching brought in. This obvious fact embarrassed no one. Times were hard and these things were understood.*

Julia KASDORF (1962, Lewistown, PA) grew up Mennonite in a small town. She lived in Brooklyn for almost a decade before returning to Pennsylvania to teach at Messiah College, then at Penn State.

Meg KEARNEY (1964, New York City) grew up in the Hudson Valley, an adopted child with two adopted siblings. She lives in New Hampshire and works at Pine Manor College in Chestnut Hill, MA.

Jane KENYON (1947–1995) grew up in Ann Arbor, a solitary child, her father a jazz pianist, her mother a singer and seamstress. She majored in English at the

University of Michigan and married her professor, Donald Hall. She moved with him to Eagle Pond Farm in New Hampshire, his ancestral home, where she began to work seriously as a poet. She died of leukemia at the age of 47.

Galway KINNELL (1927, Providence, RI) lives in Sheffield, VT. His poems are collected in 10 books, including *Flower Herding on Mount Monadnock, Body Rags*, and *The Avenue Bearing the Initial of Christ into the New World: Poems 1946–1964*. *What troubles me is a sense that so many things lovely and precious in our world seem to be dying out. Perhaps poetry will be the canary in the mine shaft warning us of what's to come.*

August KLEINZAHLER (1949, Jersey City, NJ) has worked as a locksmith, cab driver, lumberjack, music critic, teacher, and building manager. He lives in San Francisco but spends much of his time traveling, teaching and speaking. *Both familiarity and strangeness can be fruitful when it comes to writing... I'm always glad to get back to San Francisco, among my own books and music and pots and pans. So it's a conflict I've milked in the work. I love coming to New Jersey, but I love missing it too.*

William KLOEFKORN (1932, Attica, KS) is a former Marine, former state poet of Nebraska, and one-time Nebraska hog-calling champion. With his wife, Eloise, he has four children, 11 grandchildren, and two great-grandchildren. *[Poetry is] an attitude looking for something to sit on.*

Ron KOERTGE (1940, Olney, IL) lives in South Pasadena, CA. *There are supposed to be two kinds of writers: those who like to write and those who like having written. I'm the first kind. I can be the second kind.*

Ted KOOSER (1939, Ames, IA) worked for Lincoln Benefit Life in Nebraska for 35 years, rose to vice president, retired at age 60 to teach poetry, then became U.S. poet laureate, the first from the Great Plains. He lives on a farm near Garland, Nebraska, and arises early each day to write. His *Local Wonders: Seasons in the Bohemian Alps* (2002) describes southeastern Nebraska and *The Poetry Home Repair Manual* (2005) is a guidebook to the art of writing and revising poetry. *I revise toward clarity and away from difficulty, wanting the poem to appear to be written with ease.*

Maxine KUMIN (1925, Philadelphia) married an engineer, brought up children in a Boston suburb, and enrolled in an adult education poetry workshop, where she met Anne Sexton, who became her close friend. Author of five novels and more than 20 children's books, she and her husband live on a farm in New Hampshire, where they breed Arabian and quarter horses.

Kathryn KYSAR (1960, Winfield, KS) grew up in St. Paul, MN, where she lives now. She has worked as a front-desk clerk and a co-op cashier in addition to flipping burgers at McDonald's and serving beer at the State Fair. She has taught college courses in Denmark and China and currently teaches at Anoka-Ramsey Community College.

Charlie LANGDON (1934) is a columnist and senior critic for *The Durango Herald* in Colorado. He is the author of two volumes of poetry, *The Dandelion Vote* and *The Bearing Tree*, and a history of Purgatory Ski Resort, *Durango Ski*.

Gary L. LARK (1945) grew up on a small family farm in the Umpqua River Valley in southern Oregon. He has worked as a carpenter, janitor, salesman, and hospital aide, and served six years in the Army National Guard. After finishing a degree in American Studies in 1972, he harvested Christmas trees for a while before getting into the library business where he went on to work in seven different libraries. He's now retired and lives in Ashland, OR.

Dorianne LAUX (1952, Augusta, ME) has worked as a sanatorium cook, a gas station manager, a maid, and a donut holer. She lives in Raleigh, NC. *I like my poems to be understood by anyone walking down the street, waiting at a bus stop, driving a cab, waiting tables—or even a mother sitting in a hospital room with a kid who's OD'd. Unfortunately, those people read very little poetry. Even so, I write for them.*

Emma LAZARUS (1849–1887) was a Sephardic Jew and an early Zionist. She wrote the lines ("Give me your tired . . .") engraved on the Statue of Liberty.

Brad LEITHAUSER (1953, Detroit) teaches at Mount Holyoke with his wife, poet Mary Jo Salter. *As a poet, I'm very interested in structures and what you might call the mathematics of poetry, the prosody of poetry, the stuff that is as independent of meaning as anything in a poem can be independent of meaning.*

Eleanor LERMAN (1952) was born and raised in the Bronx, NY. Her father was a factory worker with aspirations to be a tap-dancing comedian. She has written short fiction, comedy, and true crime, as well as poetry. She lives on Long Island. *When I was younger, I was much too full of myself. I thought something like* well, I wrote this poem so it must be brilliant, wonderful. *I now recognize that I am a workman, and I need to build my house with care. Sometimes you pick up the wrong tool, use the wrong part so you have to start over again.*

Philip LEVINE (1928) was born in Detroit to Russian-Jewish immigrant parents. He lives in New York City and Fresno, CA, and teaches at NYU.

Gerald LOCKLIN (1941, Rochester, NY) taught at California State, Long Beach, for 42 years and still lectures there. *I didn't actually write my first poems, I composed them. I was three or four years old and one of my aunts would stand me up on the bed looking out the window at bedtime and tell me to make up a poem, and I would, and she'd write it down, and so I grew up taking it for granted that I was a writer.*

Jeanne LOHMANN lives in Olympia, WA, and is the mother of four. She has published five books of poetry and two books of prose (Fithian Press). Her collection *Thread That Sings in My Hands* won the 2003 National Looking Glass Chapbook Award, and the Olympia Poetry Network has named an annual poetry competition in her honor. Her poem is taken from the sequence titled "The Gloria Poems," found in *Calls from a Lighted House.*

Henry Wadsworth LONGFELLOW (1807–1882, Portland, ME) graduated from Bowdoin College at 19, studied languages abroad—German, Italian, French, Spanish, and Scandinavian languages—traveling the continent on foot and playing his silver flute for room and board. He became a popular and successful poet, author of best-selling book-length poems such as *Song of Hiawatha* and *Evangeline*. *In character, in manner, in style, in all the things, the supreme excellence is simplicity.*

Phillip LOPATE (1943, Brooklyn) teaches at Hofstra, Columbia, the New School, and Bennington. He lives in New York City. *Though I am known today mostly as an essayist, occasionally as a fiction writer, for about fifteen years I wrote poetry . . . When I look back at those years during which poetry formed such an important part of my identity, I am tempted to rub my eyes, as though recalling a time when I ran off and joined the circus.*

Linda McCARRISTON (1943, Lynn, MA) is a survivor of childhood sexual abuse and writes poetry to speak about that trauma. *Those who argue that poetry says the unsayable generally mean the unsayably beautiful or the unsayably profound, but the unsayable can also mean what people don't want said, ever.*

Dawn McDUFFIE (1945, Flint, MI) grew up in a large family in Milford, MI, where there were more churches than grocery stores, and decided to become a poet at age nine. She went to school in Detroit, fell in love with the city, moved there permanently in 1968, and taught high school English for 25 years. *Detroit* *is my muse. Kind neighbors, broken factories, the old lilacs that bloom every spring in the vacant lots where there used to be houses—all these places speak to me.*

Wesley McNAIR (1941, Newport, NH) grew up in public housing outside of Springfield, VT where his mother took in sewing and cut hair to support him and his two brothers. He worked on dairy farms in the Connecticut Valley, married young, taught school, was "perpetually broke and in debt," but preserved his mornings for writing poetry. He lives in Mercer, ME. *I have come to the conclusion that poets are menders of broken things.*

Freya MANFRED (1944, Minneapolis) grew up along the Minnesota River, her father a famous novelist. She spent time in California and Boston, and now lives in western Wisconsin with her husband and sons.

Dan MASTERSON (1934, Buffalo, NY) has been an actor, a disc jockey, a missionary worker, an advertising copywriter, and learned to drum by listening to 78 rpm records at 33 rpm. To this day, he carries a drum key in his right pocket, and a rosary in his left. He taught English for 46 years, and lives in Pearl River, NY. *I started writing poetry and stashing it out of sight in an orangewood box under my bed. My days began with a different wake-up call from my dad, always in rhyme, and at noon, I'd jump the back fence from the schoolyard for lunch with my mother, and talk about the new word she'd chosen from the open dictionary lying on the kitchen table.*

Sebastian MATTHEWS (1965, Chapel Hill, NC) is the son of poets William Matthews and Marie Harris, and lives in Asheville, NC. *Rarely, and these are often the best poems, a line comes unbidden to my lips. I say it to myself a few times, let it run out a little like a fishing line. I'll reel it back in, and throw it out again (usually walking along a river or heading to a cafe) to see if it will go out further. I'm not worried about catching a fish; it's the reciprocal act of casting and reeling in that counts.*

William MATTHEWS (1942–1997, Cincinnati, OH). *Auden was wrong. It's not true that poetry makes nothing happen. It tends to work its wonders in a very small arena.*

W.S. MERWIN (1927, New York City), the son of a Presbyterian minister, is a pacifist, environmentalist, and Buddhist and lives on Maui in a house built on the lip of a dormant volcano, where he preserves endangered palm trees. *[One] should always be aware that there are no rewards for writing poetry.*

Corey MESLER (1955, Niagara Falls, NY) grew up in Raleigh, TN, a "verdant carbuncle on the side of Memphis," and has worked in bookstores his entire adult life. In 2000 he and his wife, Cheryl, bought Burke's Books of Memphis, one of the oldest (1875) continuously operating independent bookstores in the country. He is the author of four novels, two volumes of short stories, a full-length poetry collection, and many, many chapbooks (which "seem to appear on my lawn like mushrooms"). He lives in Memphis with Cheryl and their children, Toby and Chloe. *We must nip in the bud all this anti-intellectual nonsense that is pervading our little country. Books are sacred, even the most profane books. Books are the utmost product of freedom of speech and the highest exemplar of man's restless and inquisitive brain.*

Carolyn MILLER (1940, Dixon, MO) is a painter, book editor, and freelance writer in San Francisco, and author of cookbooks including *Chocolate, Espresso*, and *Salt and Pepper*. *I believe that we are unfaithful to the dreams of our youth at our great peril, and that the unfulfilled desires of our younger selves can make our older selves angry, bitter, and resentful. And I believe that a need to be creative is built into humans, and that when we deny that need, we live incomplete lives.*

Mark J. MITCHELL (1955, Chicago) grew up in Southern California, studied writing and medieval literature and makes his living as a wine expert in San Francisco, tasting more than 3,000 wines a year.

Michael MORAN (1947, Allentown, PA) is a psychiatrist who lives on a small farm outside of Frankfort, KY.

Robert MORGAN (1944, Hendersonville, NC) grew up on the family farm in the Green River Valley of the Blue Ridge Mountains. He studied engineering at North Carolina State, then switched to UNC at Chapel Hill to major in English. He has written two novels set in western Carolina. He lives in Ithaca, NY, and teaches at Cornell. *My first writing teacher was the novelist Guy Owen at N.C. State. . . . One day he brought one of my stories to class, an account of visiting a great-grandmother in an old house in the mountains, and announced he had wept when he read the story. This was better praise than I had gotten in math classes, and I was hooked on writing.*

Malena MÖRLING (1965, Stockholm) grew up in southern Sweden. In 2007 she worked at the School for Advanced Research in Santa Fe, NM, on a Guggenheim Fellowship. She teaches at the University of North Carolina and New England College.

Howard MOSS (1922–1987) grew up in New York City, went off to the University of Wisconsin, then was hired by *The New Yorker* at age 26 and stayed, becoming poetry editor of the magazine until shortly before his death. When he was asked his definition of a good poem, Howard Moss said: *"One I like."*

Howard NEMEROV (1920–1991, New York City) born on Leap Day to a well-to-do New York City family, went to Harvard and under the influence of Eliot and Yeats started writing poetry. Graduated in 1942 and served as a bomber pilot in WWII and returned to the States to spend the rest of his life teaching and writing poetry. He once said he liked teaching because he could do all of his explaining in class, and that allowed him to write poetry with no explanations. He wrote several novels, including *The Melodramatists* (1949) and *The Homecoming Game* (1957).

William NOTTER (1971, Cobleskill, NY) grew up in Holyoke, CO. He spent three summers as a guide in Wyoming's Bighorn National Forest. He lives in Virginia.

Naomi Shihab NYE (1952) grew up in St. Louis, San Antonio, and Jerusalem, the daughter of a Palestinian father and an American mother. She lives in San Antonio and calls herself a "wandering poet." *[Poetry is] conversation with the world, conversation with those words on the page allowing them to speak back to you—conversation with yourself.*

Debra NYSTROM (1954, Pierre, SD) grew up in South Dakota, where her family still holds land along the Missouri River. She lives in Charlottesville, VA, and teaches creative writing at the University of Virginia.

Sharon OLDS (1942, San Francisco) was raised as a "hellfire Calvinist" in Berkeley, CA. She graduated from Stanford and earned her Ph.D. at Columbia in American Literature. After 10 years of trying to write and feeling she was only imitating other poets, she stood on the steps of the Columbia library and made a vow to Satan, saying, "I will give up all I have learned here if I can just write my own poems and I don't care if they're good. I just want to write my own stuff." She finally published her first book of poems, *Satan Says*, in 1980, when she was 37. *I was a late bloomer. But anyone who blooms at all, ever, is very lucky.*

Sheila PACKA (1956) grew up on the Iron Range in Minnesota, the granddaughter of Finnish immigrants. She majored in social work. She lives in Duluth. *It is easy for people to dismiss their secret passion and not take it seriously, but you should always do what you love.*

Grace PALEY (1922–2007, New York City) grew up in the Bronx, the daughter of Russian-Jewish immigrants. A longtime political activist, she lived in New York City and Thetford Hill, VT. *I learned whatever I know about writing and craft from writing poems.*

Greg PAPE (1947, California) lives in Stevensville, MT, where he and his wife have raised two sons and numerous free-range chickens. He has taught at the University of Montana (Missoula) since 1987. *I think that poetry needs to be demystified a bit. It's simply a sustained use of language as art—nothing more. Art and poetry help us live our lives, and everybody is a potential poet, anybody can do art.*

Linda PASTAN (1932, New York City) grew up in the Bronx and has spent most of her adult life in Potomac, MD, and lives there still. She studied poetry at Radcliffe College. *I was a product of the '50s—what I called the perfectly polished floor syndrome. I had to have a homemade dessert on the table for my husband every night . . . I stopped writing for almost ten years, and I was very unhappy about it during those years. And my husband finally said he was tired of hearing what a good poet I would have been if I hadn't gotten married.*

Alice N. PERSONS (1952, Waltham, MA) has worked as an English teacher, a legal secretary, a copy editor, and a singing waitress. She cofounded Moon Pie Press with Nancy Henry, whom she met in law school, in 2003. Alice lives in Westbrook, ME, with her husband, four cats, and a dog. *The difference between an amateur poet and a serious poet is the willingness to work at revision, but also to know when to let it go.*

Marge PIERCY (1936, Detroit) grew up poor, a white girl in a black neighborhood, started writing at 15 and became the first in her family to go to college. Her grandfather, a union organizer, had been murdered while organizing bakery workers; she became a radical feminist activist in the Sixties, getting up early in the morning to write for a few hours before spending the day and night on political causes. Her 1975 novel, *Woman on the Edge of Time*, is about a woman with Utopian visions imprisoned in a mental hospital. *I was laboring for a sense of my self, origins, prospects, antecedents, intentions, a renewed sense of a living language natural to my mouth.*

Katha POLLITT (1949, New York, NY) is a feminist political writer and columnist ("Subject to Debate" in *The Nation*). She has taught poetry at Princeton, Barnard, and the 92nd Street Y. She lives in Berlin.

Barbara RAS (1949, New Bedford, MA) has traveled widely in Latin America and lived in Costa Rica and edited a collection of Costa Rican fiction. She directs Trinity University Press in San Antonio, and in 2009 she joined a group of writers on a mission of cultural diplomacy to Tunisia and Morocco.

James REISS (1941, New York, NY) grew up in Washington Heights on the far north end of Manhattan, and in northern New Jersey. He and his wife live near Chicago.

Kenneth REXROTH (1905–1982, South Bend, IN) was born to an Indiana family of socialists and freethinkers, grew up on the South Side of Chicago. He dropped out of high school and became an autodidact, joined the radical labor movement and traveled around the country supporting himself with odd jobs. Rexroth settled in San Francisco in 1927 because, he said, *"it was not settled by Puritans but by gamblers, prostitutes, rascals, and fortune seekers."* He loved the High Sierras, rallied to the cause of Japanese Americans held in internment camps, protested all wars, promoted Ferlinghetti and other poets on his KPFA radio show and was a patron of the Beat poets of the Fifties, though he scorned the notion of Beatdom as a creation of *Time* and *Life*. *The holiness of the real is always there, accessible in total immanence.*

Theodore ROETHKE (1908–1963, Saginaw, MI) was the son of a greenhouse owner. He once said, *"I may look like a beer salesman, but I'm a poet."* He became a distinguished and beloved teacher, while struggling with bipolar disorder, an illness that put him in the hospital often throughout his life. He died of a heart attack after diving into a swimming pool while visiting friends at Bainbridge Island, WA. *What we need is more people who specialize in the impossible.*

George SANTAYANA (1863–1952) was born in Madrid to a Spanish father and Scottish mother, spent much of his life in the U.S., though he never became a citizen. He taught philosophy at Harvard. In the 1920s he settled in Rome. In 1941 he entered a Catholic hospital there and died of cancer 11 years later. *The lover knows much more about absolute good and universal beauty than the logician or theologian, unless the latter, too, be lovers in disguise.*

May SARTON (1912–1995) came to America at age four, the child of Belgian refugees. She ventured into acting, went to Paris when she was 19, turned to writing, and lived a hugely productive life: 50 books, including 19 novels, more than a dozen poetry collections, several late-life journal-memoirs, including *Journal of a Solitude* (1973). After a stroke in her mid-70s, unable to write, she dictated three more books into a tape recorder. *One must think like a hero to behave like a merely decent human being.*

Ellie SCHOENFELD (1958) grew up in Duluth, MN, and performs spoken-word poetry with her band, Warm Women of the North, in and around Duluth. *I think we poets just write stuff and other people find deep layers and complexity in it.*

Philip SCHULTZ (1945) grew up in Rochester, NY, the son of Lithuanian immigrants. He spent his 20s and 30s roaming the country before settling back in New York.

Anne SEXTON (1928–1974) grew up in comfortable surroundings in Weston, MA, which made her distinctly uneasy—her father's alcoholism, her mother's anger—a tall, beautiful, dark-haired girl (later a fashion model) who eloped at 19 and settled into a life of child-rearing, depression, and a suicide attempt on her 28th birthday. Her first collection, *To Bedlam and Part Way Back* (1960), described her breakdown and recovery. She became a famous poet, publishing four more books in quick succession, even as her life unraveled, ravaged by alcoholism and depression. *The Death Notebooks* came out in 1974, *The Awful Rowing Toward God* in 1975, a year after her suicide.

Harvey SHAPIRO (1924) served in the Air Force in WWII. *Poetry is a way of discovering what you want to say. That's different from journalism. Things should surprise you. Poetry is a kind of exploration, that's my belief.*

Faith SHEARIN (1969) has sold taffy, taught high school English, and read tea leaves. She lives with her husband and daughter in Baltimore.

Julie SHEEHAN (1964) was born and raised in Pierson, IA. She tended bar for many years. Her poems are collected in *Bar Book, Orient Point*, and *Thaw*. She lives in East Quogue, NY, with her husband, John Thorsen Jr., and their son.

Deborah SLICER (1953) is a philosopher specializing in environmental ethics and ecofeminism. She lives near Missoula, where she teaches philosophy at the University of Montana.

W.D. SNODGRASS (1926–2009) was born in Wilkinsburg, PA. He went to Geneva College and served in the U.S. Navy. His first collection of poetry was *Heart's Needle* (1959).

Gary SNYDER (1930, San Francisco) grew up on his family's subsistence farm north of Seattle. During college he worked summers as a timber scaler and fire lookout in the Cascades and on a trail crew at Yosemite. He hung out with the Beats, then spent 12 years at a Buddhist monastery in Japan. *A life that is vowed to simplicity, appropriate boldness, good humor, gratitude, unstinting work and play, and lots of walking brings us close to the actual existing world and its wholeness.*

William STAFFORD (1914–1993) grew up in Kansas. He was a conscientious objector during WWII, and did his service fighting fires and building roads in Arkansas and California. He migrated to Iowa, then to Oregon, where he taught for 32 years at Lewis and Clark College. Early every morning, he sat down with pen and paper and waited for a poem to come to him. His first major collection, *Traveling Through the Dark*, was published when he was 48 and won the National Book Award. *Poverty plus confidence equals / pioneers. We never doubted.*

Ellen STEINBAUM (1943) is a journalist, playwright, and blogger, a former *Boston Globe* columnist. She lives in Cambridge. *I used to think that creativity and boredom were mutually exclusive. Now I wonder if they're not inextricably intertwined.*

Terry STEVENSON lives in Los Angeles, and is an attorney for the city of Burbank, specializing in employment and construction law.

Joseph STROUD (1943, Glendale, CA) grew up listening to his mother's recordings of Dylan Thomas. He divides his time between Santa Cruz and a cabin in the Sierra Nevadas. *The relationship between the person and the work of art is a thorny one. What is the binding impetus of poets? It's in the writing.*

Joyce SUTPHEN (1949, Stearns County, MN) grew up on a farm near St. Joseph, MN, and teaches at Gustavus Adolphus College in St. Peter. *Here's what happens when I sit down to write a poem: I think that I will say something about this, but I end up writing about that.*

May SWENSON (1913–1989) was born in May in Logan, UT, the oldest of 10 children of Mormon parents who emigrated from Sweden, and she moved to New York City, where she could live freely as a lesbian, and was a writer-in-residence at numerous schools across the country. *Poetry is based in a craving to get through the curtains of things as they appear, to things as they are, and then into the larger, wilder space of things as they are becoming . . . Not to need illusion—to dare to see and say how things really are, is the emancipation I would like to attain.*

James TATE (1943, Kansas City, MO) has taught at Berkeley, Columbia, Emerson and UMass Amherst.

Sara TEASDALE (1884–1933) was born in St. Louis, the youngest child of wealthy, middle-aged parents, led a miserable, sheltered childhood, moved to Chicago. Vachel Lindsay courted her, but she married a rich St. Louis businessman instead, divorced him, moved to New York, took a female lover. In 1933, in poor health, alone in the city, she took an overdose of sleeping pills and died, a year after the suicide of her old lover, Vachel Lindsay. *When I can look life in the eyes, / grown calm and very coldly wise, / life will have given me the truth, / and taken in exchange my youth.*

James TRACY (1970, Oakland, CA) is a former busboy and deliveryman, now a teacher in San Francisco.

David TUCKER (1947, South Orange, NJ) grew up in Tennessee. A journalist, he lives in New Jersey.

John UPDIKE (1932–2009) born in Shillington, PA, the model for his fictional towns of Olinger and Brewer in *The Centaur* (1963) and the Rabbit Angstrom series. A generous reviewer of fiction, a graceful and hugely prolific writer, he spent more than 50 years with *The New Yorker*. *Art is like baby shoes. When you coat them with gold, they can no longer be worn.*

Mona VAN DUYN (1921–2004) grew up in Eldora, IA, a tall awkward girl, the only child of farmers, who wrote secretly in her notebooks through high school and then went off to Iowa State and the University of Iowa to become a teacher. *Most [poets] are happy to be indistinguishable in public, leading quiet, domestic lives. The private aspects of the wild and the unique are saved for the poems.*

David WAGONER (1926, Massillon, OH) is the son of a classicist who worked in the steel mills. *He was a melter. He tried to keep his brain / From melting in those tiger-mouthed mills . . . But it melted. His classical learning ran / Down and away from him, not burning bright.* David went to Penn State, studied with Theodore Roethke—later, they taught together at University of Washington. His novel *The Escape Artist* (1965) was made into a movie by Francis Ford Coppola. He teaches at the Northwest Institute of Literary Arts on Whidbey Island, WA.

Ronald WALLACE (1945) was born in Cedar Rapids, IA, and grew up in St. Louis. He and his wife live on a farm in Richland County, WI.

Julene Tripp WEAVER (1953, Callicoon, NY) lives in Seattle where she works in HIV/AIDS services. *I love time. I'm a poet, time is more valuable than money. Time is the essence of life. Time to walk, write, think, read, indulge in memories, reverie, and random threads that pull into poems.*

Walt WHITMAN (1819–1892) grew up in Brooklyn, worked as a printer, then as a newspaperman in Manhattan, loved walking up and down Broadway and around the Battery, loved tabloids. *I like limber, lashing, fierce words . . . strong, cutting, beautiful, rude words.* In 1846 he went to New Orleans and saw a slave auction, was amazed at the mixture of Spanish and English and French, and came to believe, with the prospect of a civil war, that America needed poetry to bind it together. The first edition of *Leaves of Grass* came out in 1855. A potboiler novel he had written earlier sold 20,000 copies, but the poems, despite his heavy promotion, only sold a handful. He was a volunteer nurse during the war, a passage of his life beautifully rendered in Roy Morris Jr.'s *The Better Angel: Walt Whitman in the Civil War.*

Reed WHITTEMORE (1919, New Haven) went to Yale, served in the Air Force in World War II, taught at Carleton College in Minnesota, then at the University of Maryland. *I have been impressed by the insufficiencies of the short-poem art for about twenty-five years; yet I have gone on writing short poems, and I suspect that my reputation as a poet, if I have any, is almost entirely based on a few short poems. I find the genre a congenial one in which to deal with my own insufficiencies, among which is my own rational incapacity to work things out, order them logically, on a big scale.*

Anne Pierson WIESE (1964, Minneapolis) grew up in Brooklyn. Her first collection of poems, *Floating City*, was published in 2007.

C.K. WILLIAMS (1936, Newark) began writing poetry to impress his girlfriend. He said, *"I wasn't particularly compelled by words for their own sake, or by 'literature,' which had always repelled me with its auras of mustiness and reverence. I detested almost any book I had to read, hated English in school, and I must have been surprised, maybe even a little put off, to find myself, just as the dreary poetry survey courses ended, turning the stuff out myself."* Married to a French woman, he lives part-time in Paris, part in the U.S.

William Carlos WILLIAMS (1883–1963) was born in Rutherford, NJ. His mother was Puerto Rican and read and spoke to him in Spanish. He went to school in Switzerland and France, came back for medical school, settled in Rutherford, was head pediatrician at the General Hospital in Paterson, NJ, and wrote his poems during breaks, on scraps of paper, without time to revise. *I have never felt that medicine interfered with me but rather that it was my very food and drink, the very thing which made it possible for me to write.*

Christopher WISEMAN (1936, Hull, England) came to the U.S. in 1959, married an American woman, now lives in Calgary.

Vincent WIXON (1944) grew up in rural Minnesota, and lives in Ashland, OR, where he serves as official scorekeeper for the high school baseball team.

Constance Fenimore WOOLSON (1840–1894) grew up in Cleveland, a grand-niece of James Fenimore Cooper. After her mother's death in 1879, she moved to Europe and the following year she met Henry James with whom she was rumored to have had a romance. In 1893, she moved to Venice and took an apartment on the Grand Canal. Suffering from depression, she either jumped or fell to her death from a window the following January.

Baron WORMSER (1948, Baltimore) worked as a librarian in Madison, ME, for 25 years and taught at the University there. He lives in Cabot, VT.

Charles WRIGHT (1935, Pickwick Dam, TN) grew up in eastern Tennessee. His father was an engineer for the Tennessee Valley Authority, and the family moved from dam to dam. He lives in Charlottesville and teaches at the University of Virginia. *Poets are like restaurants—as soon as they are successful, they are imitated. Really good poets are like really good restaurants—they are inimitable, though one is continually nourished there.*

James WRIGHT (1927–1980) grew up poor during the Depression in Martins Ferry, OH, his father, Dudley Wright, worked at the Hazel-Atlas Glass factory, his mother, Jesse, in a laundry, their house surrounded by smokestacks, the snowdrifts black from soot. James enlisted in the Army and went to Kenyon College on the GI Bill. *The one tongue I can write in / Is my Ohioan.*

Kevin YOUNG (1970, Lincoln, NE) grew up in Topeka, KS. He lives in Atlanta and teaches at Emory University. *I try very hard not to think about style when writing. Like Jean-Michel Basquiat said about painting, when I'm working I don't try to think about art, I try to think about life. The job of the poem is to bridge the two, to take us out of the world and hopefully deposit us back unsettled but satisfied.*

Author Index

Title Index

Copyright Acknowledgments

Poconos, Route 80, 1:30 A.M., Snow" from *Search Party: Collected Poems of William Matthews*. Copyright © 2004 by Sebastian Matthews and Stanley Plumly. Reprinted by permission of Houghton Mifflin Harcourt Publishing Company. All right reserved.

Linda McCarriston, "Riding Out at Evening" from *Talking Soft Dutch* © 1984 Texas Tech University Press. Reprinted by permission of the publisher.

Dawn McDuffie, "Motor City Tirade." First published in *Rattle*. Reprinted by permission of the author.

Wesley McNair, "Small Towns Are Passing" from *Lovers of the Lost: New & Selected Poems*. Copyright © 2010 by Wesley McNair. Reprinted by permission of David R. Godine, Inc.

W. S. Merwin, "Late Wonders" from *Flower in Hand,* in *Second Four Books of Poems*. Copyright © 1993 by W. S. Merwin. Used with permission of The Wylie Agency, LLC.

Corey Mesler, "Sweet Annie Divine" from *Short Story and Other Short Stories,* (Parellel Press, 2006). First appeared in *Strawberry Press*. Reprinted by permission of the author.

Carolyn Miller, "A Warm Summer in San Francisco" from *Light, Moving* (Sixteen Rivers Press). Copyright 2009 by Carolyn Miller. By permission of the author.

Mark J. Mitchell, "Minor League Rainout, Iowa" from *Line Drives* (Southern Illinois Press, 2002). Reprinted by permission of the author.

Michael Moran, "The Day I Made My Father Proud" from *The Fallen World*. Reprinted by permission of the author.

Robert Morgan, "Squatting" from *Topsoil Road*. Copyright © 2005 by Robert Morgan. Reprinted by permission of Louisiana State University Press.

Malena Mörling, "For Bartleby" from *Ocean Avenue*. © 1999. Reprinted with permission of New Issues Poetry & Prose.

Howard Moss, "At the Algonquin" from *New Selected Poems*. Reprinted with permission by The Estate of Howard Moss.

Howard Nemerov, "To His Piano." Used by permission.

William Notter, "Morning News in the Bighorn Mountains" from *Holding Everything Down: Poems*. Copyright © 2009 by William J. Notter IV. Reprinted by permission of Southern Illinois University Press.

Naomi Shihab Nye, "San Antonio" from *Is This Forever, or What?* Copyright © 2004 Naomi Shihab Nye. Used by permission of HarperCollins Publishers.

Debra Nystrom, "Skinny-Dipping After Work at the Drive-In" from *Bad River Road*. Copyright © 2009 by Debra Nystrom. Reprinted by permission of Sarabande Books, www.sarabande.org. All rights reserved.

Debra Nystrom, "Snow" from *Torn Sky*. Copyright © 2003 by Debra Nystrom. Reprinted by permission of Sarabande Books, www.sarabande.org.

Sharon Olds, "The Wedding Vow" from *The Unswept Room*, copyright © 2002 by Sharon Olds. Used by permission of Alfred A. Knopf, a division of Random House, Inc.

Sharon Olds, "The Elopement" from *Blood, Tin, Straw*. Copyright © 1999 by Sharon Olds. Used by permission of Alfred A. Knopf, a division of Random House, Inc.

Sharon Olds, "His Stillness" from *The Father*. Copyright © 1992 by Sharon Olds. Used by permission of Alfred A. Knopf, a division of Random House, Inc.

Sharon Olds, "Still Life in Landscape" from *Strike Sparks: Selected Poems, 1980–2002* by Sharon Olds. Copyright © 2004 by Sharon Olds. Used by permission of Alfred A. Knopf, a division of Random House, Inc.

Sheila Packa, "Driving at Night" from *The Mother Tongue*. Copyright © 2007 Sheila Packa. Reprinted by permission of the author.

Grace Paley, "In the Bus" and "Winter Afternoon" from *Begin Again: Collected Poems*. Copyright © 2000 by Grace Paley. Reprinted by permission of Farrar, Straus and Giroux, LLC.

Greg Pape, "Small Pleasures" from *American Flamingo: Poems*. © 2005 by Greg Pape. Reprinted by permission of Southern Illinois University Press.

Linda Pastan, "25th High School Reunion" from *The Five Stages of Grief*. Copyright © 1978 by Linda Pastan. Used by permission of W. W. Norton & Company, Inc.

Linda Pastan, "Notes from the Delivery Room," from *AM/PM: New and Selected Poems*. Copyright © 1971 by Linda Pastan. Used by permission of W. W. Norton & Company, Inc.

Alice N. Persons, "Why I Have a Crush on You, UPS Man" and "Meadowbrook Nursing Home" from *Don't Be A Stranger* (Sheltering Pines Press). Copyright 2007 by Alice N. Persons. By permission of the author.

Marge Piercy, "Motown, Arsenal of Democracy" from *The Crooked Inheritance*. Copyright © 2006 by Middlemarsh, Inc. Used by permission of Alfred A. Knopf, a division of Random House, Inc.

Katha Pollitt, "The Old Neighbors" from *The Mind-Body Problem: Poems*, copyright © 2009 by Katha Pollitt. Used by permission of Random House, Inc.

Katha Pollitt, "Ballet Blanc" from *Antarctic Traveller*. Copyright © 1981 by Katha Pollitt. Used by permission of Alfred A. Knopf, a division of Random House, Inc.

Barbara Ras, "A Wife Explains Why She Likes Country" from *One Hidden Stuff*. Copyright © Barbara Ras, 2006. Used by permission of Penguin Books, a member of Penguin Group (USA) Inc.

James Reiss, "My Daughters in New York" from *Ten Thousand Good Mornings*. Copyright ©